Stravinsky

ROBERT SIOHAN
Translated by Eric Walter White

Stravinsky

GROSSMAN PUBLISHERS, NEW YORK 1970

Stravinsky

by ROBERT SIOHAN

Contents

Karsavina, Nijinsky, Pavlova

Introduction

In the annals of art, the figure of Igor Stravinsky appears as one of the rare examples of a creative artist who, starting with an early group of works that shook music to its foundations with their strangeness and originality, appeared like an explosive force on the musical scene—a magnificent figure according to some, a chaotic and abortive influence according to others—but an artist who later on repented of the error of his ways and, leaving most of his contemporaries to follow the trail he had already blazed, unexpectedly and almost incredibly became an active defender of law, order and tradition. And so the creator of *The Rite of Spring*—whose career is in many ways comparable with that of Pablo Picasso—appears as something of an enigma; and when it is remembered that, like the painter of *Guernica*, Stravinsky, despite violent and sarcastic attacks, has been recognised for more than half a century as one of the great masters of contemporary music, it becomes all the more desirable to examine and scrutinise this figure in the hope of discovering his secret and relating him and his works to the world of the twentieth century.

Such is the main purpose of this book; and since it is going to outline the capricious progression of Stravinsky's music, it is bound to touch on various events, some of minor, others of major importance, that occurred during his lifetime which covers what has undoubtedly been one of the most troubled periods in the history of the world, including the two World Wars and a number of revolutions.

It is true that Stravinsky has always turned away from the harsh actuality of major political events in an attempt to construct his own universe of music outside the subjective battlefield of passions and emotions. Nevertheless, it will be seen that the impact of events, exercising their influence as it were at a distance, has affected the orbit of his private universe, for music which by its essence is perhaps the most abstract of all the arts can hardly even in its purest state be completely divorced from human considerations.

Youth

Youth

On the south side of the Gulf of Finland, just opposite the fortress of Cronstadt, is the little town of Oranienbaum with its baroque palace and the luxuriant vegetation of its park and its hundred-year-old oaks. Situated only a few miles from the former capital of the Tsars of Russia, this town with a population of 7,000 formed one of the favourite country residences of the St. Petersburg upper classes towards the end of the nineteenth century, and it was here that the well-known opera singer, Fedor Ignarevitch Stravinsky, had his country house. Perhaps he found that, after the turmoil of the winter season in St. Petersburg, this place reminded him of the country scenes in which his youth had been spent, for he was of Polish descent and came from an important family of landowners.

His career had brought him quickly to the top of his profession. Fresh from the St. Petersburg Conservatory, he had spent the three years 1873-6 at the Kiev Opera House. On his return to the capital, he joined the Imperial Opera Company and, thanks to his considerable talents as a comic actor, soon acquired a well-deserved reputation. Although his bass voice lacked natural beauty of timbre, he succeeded through his intelligence and capacity for hard work in developing it into a well-trained organ. In an attempt to avoid dead routine in his acting, he carried on the tradition of O. A. Petrov, one of the creators of the Russian realistic style in the theatre, and with equal mastery succeeded in interpreting diametrically opposite characters, which meant that his

◀ *The Window in the Country* (*Chagall*, 1915) *Tretiakov Gallery, Moscow*

Igor's parents: Feodor and Anne

repertory was an exceptionally large one. Among his favourite roles were Holophernes and Eramka in Serov's *Judith*, and Golova in Rimsky-Korsakov's *Night of May* and *The Night Before Christmas*. Sometimes he played Varlam and sometimes Rangoni in *Boris Godunov*, and he was equally at home in the works of Tchaikovsky, including *The Enchantress*, *Mazeppa* and *The Maid of Orleans*, where he gave authoritative performances of the roles of Massirev, Orlic and de Dunois. His wide culture made it easy for him to tackle the repertory of foreign operas and he appeared as Mephistopheles in Gounod's *Faust*, Marcel in *Les Huguenots* and Don Bartolo or Don Basilio in *The Barber of Seville*.

It was during one of his periods of residence at Oranienbaum that his son, Igor Feodorovich, was born—on 18th June, 1882 (or 5th June according to the old Greek Calendar). A photograph taken a year later shows a chubby baby, seated somewhat precariously on an easy chair, with a determined look in his eye. Perhaps an echo of some of the child's first impressions is to be found in the Three Little Songs written thirty years later with their subtitle 'Memories of My Childhood'. His niania may have sung him to sleep with a lullaby like *The Magpie* or *The Rook*. Perhaps also, when writing the Fair Scene in *Petrushka*, he recalled the *Katalnaia Gorka* (the scenic railways) that he saw as a little boy in the Imperial Park of his native town.

One thing is certain. From his earliest years, the young Igor lived in an atmosphere of music, whether it was the unison songs of the villagers of Oranienbaum, redolent of the soil, or the cultivated music of opera, fragments of which would penetrate the walls of his room during the long winters in St. Petersburg.

At the age of nine, having begun to study the piano, he was allowed to attend some of the numerous musical parties that took place in his parents' house. His progress was very rapid, and quite soon, although he received no encouragement from his family, he started to improvise. He loved reading opera scores; and after attending a performance of *A Life for the Tsar* (his first visit to the theatre and his first experience of an orchestra) he returned home dazzled by Glinka's light, transparent orchestration.

Igor aged five years

It was in another opera of Glinka's, *Ruslan and Ludmilla*, that he first saw his father on the stage in the part of Farlav, which was one of the best in his repertory. After the performance he was allowed to go behind the scenes, and there the future composer of *The Fairy's Kiss* caught a glimpse of Tchaikovsky shortly after the first performance of the Pathetic Symphony and a fortnight before his sudden death from cholera.

As a boy Igor paid little attention to his work at school, being fully occupied with his own interests and attending opera performances and concerts as often as he could. What he wanted above all was to acquire sufficient technical proficiency to become a composer, and he devoted himself to this task—or, rather, this diversion—with an enquiring spirit that frequently resulted in the satisfaction of having discovered things for himself. In his book, *Chronicle of My Life* he wrote: 'I always did, and still do, prefer to achieve my aims and to solve any problems which confront me in the course of my work solely by my own efforts, without having recourse to established processes which do, it is true, facilitate the task, but which must first be learnt and then remembered.'*

*Chronicle of My Life by Igor Stravinsky. London, 1936.

The Bolshoi Theatre, St. Petersburg (Alexandre Benois)

This latter remark seems to refer to his harmony studies, which gave him scant satisfaction, whereas he enjoyed wrestling with the mysteries of counterpoint. Henceforward, this capacity for self-instruction was going to awaken one of the future composer's dominant characteristics —his tendency to be always on the watch for a problem to be solved— and at the same time it showed the vigorous nature of his creative gifts, for such a method of working, if it is to be successful, presupposes the existence of a compelling internal impulse.

At the beginning of the twentieth century Stravinsky was eighteen. He was reading law, but did not allow his legal studies, undertaken without enthusiasm, to interfere with his musical vocation. Quite the contrary! But at least they furnished a convenient pretext for him to meet Rimsky-Korsakov's son, Vladimir, who became a close friend, thereby breaking a certain misanthropic tendency that had shown itself where the rest of Stravinsky's fellow students were concerned. Such a friendship was destined to be a particularly valuable one, because it was to affect his career as a musician.

At this period, Rimsky-Korsakov, who had just finished the score of *Tsar Saltan*, was held in specially high esteem by the young people of Stravinsky's generation; and as this feeling was shared by Stravinsky himself, he was naturally anxious to meet the great composer. A favourable opportunity occurred during the summer of 1902, which the Stravinsky family spent at Bad Wildungen, a little spa near Heidelberg where Rimsky-Korsakov was also staying with his family. Taking advantage of this opportunity, Igor begged Vladimir to introduce him to his father. Vladimir did so; and Rimsky-Korsakov listened with friendly interest to the young man's essays in composition, but doubtless not wishing to abandon his usual pedagogical reserve, showed himself guarded in his comments. As Stravinsky was already twenty and too old to enter the Conservatory, it seemed best for him to continue his harmony lessons with one of Rimsky-Korsakov's pupils.

Was this the result Stravinsky had expected from the meeting he had looked forward to with such eagerness? It hardly mattered one way or another, for now the way was open and the decision irrevocably taken. He was to become a composer.

'MIR ISKUSTVA'

In the last decade of the nineteenth century, a small group of *avant-garde* artists was formed in St. Petersburg, who were passionately interested in the problems of painting, music, theatre and literature. Among these enthusiastic young men, many of whom (such as Nicholas Roerich, Alexander Benois and Leon Bakst) later became famous, was Serge de Diaghilev; and this strange character was destined to follow an extraordinary career. Though neither a painter nor a writer himself, he suc-

ceeded in becoming the leading spirit of the group, and when in 1898 it was decided to found an art magazine, it seemed to everyone the most natural course to turn to Diaghilev and invite him to direct it. He owed this extraordinary ascendancy—unusual in the case of an amateur surrounded by professionals—not only to a certain resemblance to Peter the Great (of which he was particularly proud), but also to an exceptionally faithful visual memory, coupled with remarkable intuitive powers which enabled him to identify at the first glance either the author or the subject of a painting about whose identity artists themselves were frequently in doubt. In the long run, this astonishing flair of his became one of his greatest assets.

Until the age of twenty-three, Diaghilev had concentrated mainly on music. The country property of Bikbarda where he spent the greater part of his youth was the artistic centre of that particular region—'the Athens of Perm' as it was called. A musical circle was formed there; and in 1882, when Diaghilev was a boy of ten, he was able to hear performances by an amateur orchestra conducted by his uncle Vanya. Its rehearsals were held in the rooms of this vast country house, the centre of an estate of 16,000 hectares, which was run on a luxurious scale that rivalled the palace of some feudal prince. Small wonder that when the young boy grew up he wanted to become a composer; but his aspirations were checked by the unfavourable opinion of his music master Rimsky-Korsakov.

Subsequently, various visits paid to different countries in Europe helped to develop his interest in paintings, and in 1897 his first public undertaking, an exhibition of English and German water-colourists, proved a decisive success. During the next eight years, for part of which (1899-1901) he held the post of Assistant to the Director of the Imperial Theatres, he divided his activity between organising exhibitions of paintings, both in St. Petersburg and abroad, and editing the magazine *Mir Iskustva* ('The World of Art') which reflected his enthusiasms and exercised considerable influence on the Russian artistic and cultural life of that period.

It is easy to understand how at a moment when all St. Petersburg was interested in this artistic and intellectual movement, the young twenty-year-old composer Stravinsky, whose father had just died, was keen to join this group of artists who were bursting with new ideas. That he succeeded in doing so was due to his close relationship with the Rimsky-Korsakov household, where he was a frequent visitor. At the same time, his friend Ivan Pokrovsky, with the help of two members of the *Mir Iskustva* group, had just founded a series of evening concerts devoted to performances of contemporary chamber music. Recalling this period in later years, Stravinsky wrote:—★ 'It is needless to speak of the importance of these two groups in my artistic and intellectual evolution, and how much they strengthened the development of my creative faculty.'

Naturally enough, fierce hostility broke out between the supporters of the *avant-garde* movement and the guardians of *l'art officiel*. Neither the Academy nor the Imperial Society for the Encouragement of the Fine Arts could approve the activities of these young enthusiasts, whom they looked on as dangerous enemies. Rimsky-Korsakov himself, speaking of Claude Debussy, said: 'Better not listen to him; one runs the risk of getting accustomed to him and one would end by liking him.' And Debussy's works, together with those of other French contemporary composers such as Vincent d'Indy, Paul Dukas and Gabriel Fauré, were systematically banned from the St. Petersburg symphony orchestra programmes. Stravinsky was naturally not slow to familiarise himself with the hitherto ostracised scores of the new French school, which Kussevitsky and Ziloti now undertook to introduce to a Russian audience; and at the same time, being anxious to master the technique of his profession, he readily submitted himself to the discipline imposed by Rimsky-Korsakov, who from 1903 onwards took it upon himself to teach him the constructional processes that underly classical forms. The first fruit of these studies was an unpublished Piano Sonata written during 1903-4.

★*Chronicle of My Life.*

PUPIL OF RIMSKY-KORSAKOV

This was a period of great tribulation for the Russian people. The Japanese War, which broke out in 1904, led to a series of heavy defeats —from the disaster of Port Arthur to the battle of Moukden (25th February/10th March, 1905) and the annihilation of the Baltic Fleet at Tsou-shima (14th/27th—15th/28th May, 1905). The resultant weakening of the prestige of the Imperial régime produced a favourable climate for the outbreak of the revolutionary forces that had so long been simmering underground. The assassination of Plehve the Minister of the Interior in July 1904, the rising that cost the Grand-Duke Serge, Governor of Moscow, his life the following year, and the general strike which broke out in Moscow and St. Petersburg in October 1905, led to the bloody and brutal butchery of the Red Sunday (9th/22nd January, 1906), an event which deeply disturbed enlightened opinion and led to the union of all the forces opposing the Government, whether working-class or intellectual.

Although Rimsky-Korsakov was always particularly reserved in matters outside the sphere of music, he referred to this troubled period in his autobiography in the following terms: 'Already before the Christmas holidays it was plain that the students were seething with excitement. . . . On 9th January a wave of political fervour swept through St. Petersburg, and the Conservatoire students were caught up in it too. . . . In the eyes of the conservative professors and those responsible for the direction of the St. Petersburg section, I appeared to be the head of the revolutionary element among the students.' He was forced to resign his post of Director; and as a result he immediately became the object of many spontaneous manifestations of sympathy—letters, newspaper articles, and a special concert of his works organised by the Conservatoire students and interrupted by the police. 'The public,' he said, 'turned to me because in this way it wished to express its dissatisfaction with the régime.'

What was Stravinsky's attitude during those tragic days? It can only be guessed at, because at no point does he mention it in his published writings. All he says in his Chronicle is that having finished his University course in the spring of 1905, he became engaged to his cousin Catherine Nossenko in the autumn and married her in January 1906.

Nevertheless, it should be noticed that not only did he continue to keep in touch with Rimsky-Korsakov, but that by now the famous master and young student had a warm mutual affection for each other. Stravinsky's Symphony in B flat minor (opus 1), finished in 1907, was dedicated to 'my dear teacher N. A. Rimsky-Korsakov.' This conventional work was preceded in 1905-6 by three pieces for voice and orchestra, *Faun and Shepherdess*, settings of poems by Pushkin, and followed in December 1907 by Two Melodies, settings for voice and piano of two poems by S. Gorodetzky which he had presumably chosen for their mystical qualities.

This output was nothing more than might have been expected from the usual Prix de Rome scholar, provided with a good academic grounding based on Schumann and Gounod, tricked out with occasional handfuls of augmented fifths naively borrowed from Debussy. But the *Scherzo Fantastique*, which dates from 1908, deserves closer attention. The first thing to notice is that, being inspired by Maeterlinck's book *The Life of the Bees*, it naturally shows a tendency towards descriptive music.* This fact will assume a special significance when later on Stravinsky's work comes to be assessed on a broader basis. According to Paul Collaer, the symmetrical form of the Scherzo symbolises the eternal renewal of the biological cycle: the swarming of the bees, the queen's nuptial flight, the love fight with her chosen mate and after his death the return of the queen and the continuing activity of the hive.

The handling of the orchestra—in the manner of Rimsky-Korsakov—shows real ability, especially in the two Con Moto movements that frame the central Moderato. This middle section which features a distinctive musical phrase that passes through various transpositions is much less successful. Nevertheless, although in this work the composer's musical personality was still in an embryonic state of development, the Scherzo was sufficiently impressive to attract the attention of Diaghilev when he heard it at one of the Ziloti Concerts in the course of the winter of 1908-9.

Meanwhile, Stravinsky was trying to find other ways in which he

*This has now been denied by Stravinsky himself. In *Conversations with Igor Stravinsky*, he tells Robert Craft that he wrote the Scherzo as a piece of 'pure' symphonic music, and the bees were a choreographer's idea. (Translator's note.)

might release the forces he felt seething inside him. In collaboration with S. Mitusov, a friend of his, he sketched out the libretto for an opera, *The Nightingale*, based on the well-known fairy tale of Hans Andersen. 'This work,' writes Stravinsky in his Chronicle, 'was greatly encouraged by my master, and to this day I remember with pleasure his approval of the preliminary sketches of these compositions.' [*i.e.* the *Scherzo Fantastique* and *The Nightingale*.] 'It grieves me much that he was never to hear them in their finished form, for I think he would have liked them.'

During the winter of 1907–8, Rimsky-Korsakov's health began to fail, and he suffered from attacks of angina. Before leaving St. Petersburg for his country estate of Ustilug in Volhynia, Stravinsky visited him with his wife and told him about a short orchestral fantasy he proposed to write during the vacation. Having finished this new work a month later, he sent it off as a present for the wedding of Rimsky-Korsakov's daughter which was about to take place. Unfortunately, the parcel containing the manuscript was returned to Stravinsky unopened. Rimsky-Korsakov had died just before it could be delivered.

This orchestral fantasy, which is dedicated to N. and M. Steinberg (Rimsky-Korsakov's daughter and son-in-law), proved to be a land-mark in Stravinsky's output. *Fireworks* uses simple means to achieve in a comparatively short time an extraordinary impression of dynamic power, and this was bound to make a powerful impact on its first audiences. After a fairly long introduction during which a whirling figure for the woodwind, somewhat reminiscent of the opening of the Revolution Scene in *Boris Godunov*, builds up orchestral tension, the single theme blazes out and is echoed and re-echoed by the brass, leading to a rapidly ascending passage which suddenly stops dead. A slow episode, closely related to the introduction of Dukas's *L'Apprenti Sorcier*, leads to a flowing passage followed by a chromatic bridge passage. After this brief moment of comparative calm, everything starts to crackle and spin again, and after two appearances of the subject cancrizans, it bursts forth more brilliantly than ever, thanks to an adroit tonal change, to finish in a final radiant explosion.

Diaghilev's infallible flair was not likely to desert him at a moment like this. Clearly the composer of such a successful work was bound to have a most promising future. He forthwith charged Stravinsky, and a number of other Russian composers, with the task of instrumenting some of Chopin's piano pieces for the ballet *Les Sylphides* which the Russian Ballet was planning to include in its initial Paris season in the summer of 1909. Stravinsky was delighted and immediately set to work on the two pieces that had been handed over to him, though he was naturally impatient to get back to his opera *The Nightingale*, the com-position of which had been interrupted after the first act by these other works.

Meanwhile, wishing to pay homage to his dead master, he wrote a

Funeral Dirge during the summer of 1908; and this was included in the programme of the first of the Belaiev Concerts in the autumn, which was dedicated to Rimsky-Korsakov's memory. As the manuscript score has disappeared, the only record of this work, which Stravinsky has been unable to reconstruct from memory, is contained in his Chronicle. 'All the solo instruments of the orchestra filed past the tomb of the master in succession, each laying down its own melody as its wreath against a deep background of *tremolo* murmurings simulating the vibrations of bass voices singing in chorus.'

Work on *Pastorale*, (1908), a song without words for voice and piano —the last work of Stravinsky's that Rimsky-Korsakov saw—and Four Studies for Piano (1908), continued to hold up progress with *The Nightingale*; and when he returned to his desk at Ustilug in the summer of 1909, the opera had to be shelved once more in favour of a new project.

DIAGHILEV'S RUSSIAN BALLET

So far Diaghilev had shown himself to be interested primarily in painting; but, with his enthusiastic nature, he was not the sort of man to be satisfied by concentrating on a single activity. In fact, even before *Mir Iskustva* folded up in 1904 because of financial difficulties, he had been losing interest in the magazine. In his perpetual search for novelty, he was looking for new avenues to explore. He devoted some time to the idea of creating a museum of national art; but when this project proved abortive, his attention turned to the theatre. During the period when he was connected with the direction of the Imperial Theatres, he had not

Diaghilev and Ginsberg (Picasso)

only gained a knowledge of the stage, but also made a number of friends among the dancers. In matters concerning singers and the interpretation of their roles, stage settings and production, he had ideas of his own which led him, among other things, to launch a campaign to sweep away the superannuated traditions that the Imperial Theatre had inherited from Bayreuth; and in this he was so successful that in 1903 Benois and Korovine were commissioned to design the scenery for a new production of *The Twilight of the Gods*.

These were the stages by which Diaghilev was led to undertake the extremely hazardous enterprise of touring Russian opera abroad; and this led to the thrilling revelation in Paris in 1908 of Mussorgsky's masterpiece *Boris Godunov* with the virtuoso singer Chaliapin in the title role.

The following year Diaghilev succeeded in realising a project which was still at the moment only partly formulated in his mind and which

Chaliapin in the title role of Boris Godunov

in the event was destined to revolutionise the esthetics of the ballet by unifying the visual and spatial arts i.e. costume and scenery, with the temporal arts of music and choreography.

The first season of the Russian Ballet at the Théâtre du Châtelet, in 1909, made an extraordinary impression. For the first time Paris saw Pavlava, Nijinsky, Karsavina, Fokine and Ida Rubinstein; and the audiences were dazzled, not only by the freshness and splendour of the spactacle, the grace and technical brilliance of all these stars, but especially by the feeling of unity produced by the productions as a whole, the different elements of which, though immensely varied in themselves, fitted so harmoniously together.

No sooner was Diaghilev back in St. Petersburg than without a moment's delay he plunged into preparations for the following season, which he was determined should surpass the first in brilliance and novelty. To revive in Paris what Russia had inherited from France and what France had gradually forgotten, namely, the classical ballet, and also to introduce contemporary art to revivify the traditions of the ballet—these were the two main preoccupations, the one complementary to the other, that guided him in drawing up his programme.

While it was relatively simple to realise the first part of his project with *Giselle* and a new ballet that Fokine had recently produced privately, based on Schumann's *Carnaval*, the choice of modern Russian works proved much more ticklish. In addition to Rimsky-Korsakov's *Sheherazade*, it was thought there should be a fairy-tale fantasy based on the legend of the Fire Bird. At first Liadov was sounded about the commission; but when this proposal fell through, Diaghilev recalled the *Fireworks* piece that had so impressed him at one of the recent Ziloti Concerts and, feeling sure that Stravinsky was one of the most promising young Russian composers, commissioned him to write the new score. Stravinsky at this stage was still unaware of his own capabilities and felt alarmed at having to work to a fixed date. But at the same time he was flattered at being chosen by so important an impresario as Diaghilev to collaborate with such brilliant artists, and he decided to accept the challenge.

Karasavina, who originally danced the part of the Fire Bird, has given a particularly attractive portrait of Stravinsky as a young man, which shows him not only behind the scenes in the theatre, but also as a welcome guest in the best houses of St. Petersburg. 'From the way in which this young man wore his top hat tilted on the back of his head, he might have been taken for a dandy. Nevertheless, this first impression was dispelled by the unaccustomed tranquility and depth of his eyes behind their thick rimless spectacles. . . . As soon as he started to speak about music or to express himself with emphasis, he illustrated his meaning with repeated incisive movements of his head and hands—movements which, though derived from the elegant manners of a man of the world, had something spontaneous and primitive about them.'* While he showed himself anxious to learn, the young composer, though a newcomer to the theatre, had something to contribute of his own, and this was realised by those who were older and more experienced than himself. He brought a new outlook which had an effect on the work of all the members of the company. 'How interesting it was,' says Karsavina, 'to see him at the piano. His body seemed to vibrate to the rhythm of his own music.' Indeed, he often came to the theatre before the actual hour of rehearsal in order to help Karsavina by demonstrating the different tempi, explaining the rhythms, playing and replaying with inexhaustible patience difficult passages, in order to guide her through the mazes of the complicated score.

At the same time, tribute should be paid to Karsavina's modesty. She was the first to recognise the deficiencies of her musical education, superficially built up on commonplace rhythms and on tunes that were easy to memorise because they were common currency. It is a fundamental weakness of choreography as an art that, though based on the duration of the musical phrase, it continues to ignore the most elementary details of musical prosody. There is a great gulf fixed between music and dance; and if this is not successfully bridged, the art of gesture and movement instead of fulfilling its latent powers of development will continue to stagnate in its present dreary routine.

It is easy to guess at the confusion and even opposition caused by the introduction of Stravinsky's lively but complex rhythms into the ordinary ballet world; and it was in this atmosphere that the persistence of Karsavina, who had indisputably gained the rank of a star as a result of her dancing during the first Russian Ballet season in Paris, served as a powerful example. Thanks to her good offices, to the almost dictatorial authority of Diaghilev and to the prestige that Stravinsky already possessed despite his youth, *The Fire Bird*, as conceived by Fokine and realised with his imaginative choreography, began to spread its wings, which were to carry it from the cold winter of its native land to Paris in the spring.

PARIS OF THE 'BELLE EPOQUE'

If one is to believe various historians who have dealt with the events of the years round about 1905, the Paris of President Fallières—which was the Paris Diaghilev became acquainted with when he organised his remarkable Exhibition of Russian Art at the Salon d'Automne—was no longer, properly speaking, the Paris of the '*Belle Epoque*'. The international horizon had clouded over as a result of the Tangiers incident, and the law separating the Church from the State had given rise to disorders throughout the country. Nevertheless, if it is remembered that the Dreyfus case which had dragged on for about twelve years had

Tränenreiches Lernen by Tamara Karsavina. Musik der Zeit, Bonn, 1952.

provoked the most violent feelings, breaking up friendships, disrupting families, it will be realised that the conception of a '*Belle Epoque*' was to some extent based on a partial and biassed attitude, and may even have been the result of superficial judgement. Smart society considered it fashionable to lament the passing of the age of carriages, so convenient for dresses with sweeping trains and picture hats decorated with feathers; furbelows and flounces became more ridiculous as the new methods of locomotion developed, horse buses gradually giving way to trams and, later, the motorbus. Even the fashionable Bois was invaded by De Dions and Panhards, their high-backed bodies upholstered with shining leather, which kept to the crown of the road and were the precursors of '*le chic anglais*' and the taste for '*le sport*'—expressions unknown to the man of the street in the France of the nineteenth century. The sumptuous entertaining of persons like Montesquiou and Boni de Castellane— almost insolent in its flaunting luxury—played a not unimportant part in building up the concept of '*la Belle Epoque*', and perhaps also the hectic pursuit of hidden pleasures (so well portrayed by an artist like Toulouse-Lautrec) in the resorts of Montmartre and little bars of Argenteuil, to the strains of '*La Valse Brune*', '*La Très Moutarde*' and '*Ell'avait un' jamb' de bois*'. In short, the twentieth century, which seemed to be making a delayed appearance, could hardly have been distinguished from its predecessor apart from minor changes in fashion and traffic, had it not been for the rapid progress of mechanisation and the far-reaching consequences of the conquest of the air.

As far as this monograph is concerned, all this was merely the background to the development of the arts. At the Théâtre de L'Oeuvre, Lugné Poe started to build up a public for advanced drama; and informed taste began to turn away from the '*boulevard*' pieces of the two Henris—Henri Bernstein and Henri Bataille. In literature, those who pinned their faith to Maeterlinck and Anatole France had no time for Paul Bourget or René Bazin. But d'Annunzio still enjoyed the same sort of flashy prestige as a Renaissance prince, despite the growing anti-romantic tendencies. And perhaps it is true to say that this anti-romanticism, which was soon to be confirmed and accentuated by the events of the first World War, was the first real stand that the twentieth century made against the powerful esthetic traditions of the nineteenth century.

The course of this artistic evolution was dominated by the powerful personality of Pablo Picasso, whose work was just becoming known. His rejection of romantic pathos is apparent in his paintings of the rose period, which, though not necessarily more abstract in feeling than those of the blue period (1901-1905), allow the transmission of feelings which despite the painter's classical reserve are the direct result of the impact made on him by the miseries and splendours of the life of ordinary men and women working in surroundings like a fairground or circus. It was not until he had reached his negro period that he started to break down the subject matter of his paintings, a development that led step by step from cubism to abstract painting. But it should be noted that Cézanne, whose death occurred just at this time (1906), looked on his own paintings as being a kind of 'plastic equivalent of the natural motif',* so that he may be held to be the first artist who liberated painting from its bondage to subject matter, his procedure being to use the '*motif*' as a point of departure for the construction of a pictorial world made up of lines and planes, living an autonomous esthetic life of its own, quite apart from that of the natural world.

Painters like Cézanne and Picasso were not merely objects of Stravinsky's admiration. Their cast of thought was sympathetic to him and, by confirming his natural disposition, helped him to adopt a similar attitude to theirs regarding the relationship of works of art to the outside world. The curious thing about all this was that, to begin with, this identity of esthetic views was achieved solely through the intermediary of the paintings themselves. Stravinsky had no opportunity of knowing Cézanne; nor did he meet Picasso until 1917.

While the greater part of the French music-lovers at this time was devoted to Wagner, a small group of enthusiasts looked on Gabriel Fauré, Claude Debussy and the young Maurice Ravel as the leaders of a

Initiation à l'oeuvre de Picasso by Maurice Gieure.

French musical renaissance. It was these devotees who hailed *Pelléas et Mélisande* in 1902 and *La Mer* in 1905 as masterpieces; and this was a music that was closely allied by its refined sensuality to the art of the impressionists. It is true that Fauré's music was becoming increasingly refined and tending towards a kind of Attic purity; but it should be remembered that *La Bonne Chanson* belongs to 1891 and the second quartet to 1885, the first (written in 1879) having preceded *Parsifal* by three years. Although these works of Fauré's belong to the nineteenth century, they are completely fresh and display a classical reserve that contrasts strongly with the tin-pot idiom of *The Ring* and the torrential

▲
The Family of Harlequin, Picasso, 1905. (*Coll. Lewisohn, New York*)

passion of Isolde, whose stormy outpourings have no point in common with the discreet modesty of the real Yseut of the Middle Ages.

Erik Satie had just provoked considerable scorn with his *Morceaux en forme de poire*. Paul Dukas had produced *Ariane et Barbe-Bleue*; Florent Schmitt, *Psaume XLVI* and *La Tragédie de Salomé*. So there was a brilliant assemblage of French musical talent to applaud the success of *The Fire Bird* and to hail as their peer a Russian composer who had been more or less unknown until he arrived in Paris for the Russian Ballet's second season in 1910. It is no exaggeration to say that Stravinsky became famous overnight.

Shrove Tuesday, Paul Cézanne (Museum of Modern Western Art, Moscow)

Drop-curtain by Chagall for 'The Firebird'

AN ORIENTAL FAIRY TALE

Unlike *Fireworks* which is a successful apprentice composition, *The Fire Bird* is the fully fledged work of a master composer. It is true that some years later critics who examined the score would point to various influences—Glinka, Scriabin, and even Wagner—and that at an even later date, when it could be assessed in the light of his major works, it might be considered by some to rank no higher than the 'visiting card' of a young composer of twenty-eight. Nevertheless there is no doubt that it had a very different significance at the moment it appeared.

In this oriental story, everything was treated as a pretext for a lively, sumptuous spectacle, and the audience's eyes and ears were enchanted by the irresistible appeal of the ballet as a complete work of art. The scintillating bird that hovers round the fairy tree in an attempt to gather the golden apples glimpsed in the silver light of the moon may be thought to symbolise the life of man, shot through with vanity, replete with desire. Ivan, the handsome hunter, full of youthful fire, pursues the bird which always eludes him. Nevertheless, he manages to retain as talisman a golden feather, which ultimately helps him to vanquish fear, the enemy of all human initiative, personified by the immortal ogre Kashchei, the revolting giant with green claws who petrifies all who come within his grasp. Ivan obtains possession of Kashchei's soul in the shape of an egg and deliberately breaks it, thereby releasing the captive princesses (who are really his thoughts in disguise); and the most beautiful of these becomes his bride, and the enchanted castle is filled with rejoicing.

The score, which ingeniously combines contrasted moods of mystery with splendour, charm with barbaric frenzy, immediately captivated its audience and held it spellbound; and the critics were just as enthusiastic as the public, some of them being carried away by the surface richness of this lively, glittering music, while others were impressed by its formal strength, due to its symphonic structure, and its polyphonic ingenuity —qualities that were rarely to be found at that time in music written to accompany ballet.

The day after the unforgettable première of 25th June, 1910, Alfred Bruneau summarised the general feeling as follows:* 'Here at last is a work that is absolutely beautiful, completely new and deeply significant. . . . I know of nothing else in the art of ballet which is likely to prove so memorable as this.' These were certainly prophetic words.

If one examines the musical content of the ballets of that period, they fall into two main divisions: on the one hand there were scores that were not intended to be used for choreography at all, such as Rimsky-Korsakov's *Sheherazade* and *Les Sylphides* after Chopin, adaptations that were always bound to betray the composer's original intentions; on the other hand, there were certain brilliant pieces like the Polovtsian Dances of *Prince Igor*, which nevertheless did not rise above the level of folklore. None of these achieved the sort of musical unity that comes from the successful development of a given subject. While in Russia only the ballets of Tchaikovsky and Glazounov could be set against Stravinsky's score, it must be admitted that in France there had been nothing for a long time that it could be measured against. Because of its incontestable musical qualities, *The Fire Bird* helped to revive a declining art form; and its historical importance will be appreciated if it is remembered that, thanks to its example, ballet took on a new lease of life.

At the same time one should not ignore the contributions made by Golovine, who designed the scenery and costumes, and Fokine who was responsible for the scenario and the satisfactory working out of the action. The sense of unity produced by this incomparable partnership was so emphatic that one might have thought it to be due to a single person, and indeed Henri Ghéon wrote, 'For me, Stravinsky, Fokine and Golovine are but a single name.' But Golovine and Fokine were already favourites with the Parisian public. For Stravinsky, *The Fire Bird* was his first great public success.

HIERATIC INTERLUDE

'A fresh bout of work—that's the best form of recreation,' said Ernest Renan at the Académie Française when taking part in editing the Dictionary. In the same way, Stravinsky refreshed himself after the labours of the 1910 season by setting Two Poems of Verlaine during his short

*Le Matin, 26th June, 1910.

31

summer holiday at La Baule—*La Lune Blanche* from 'La Bonne Chanson' and *Un Grand Sommeil Noir* from 'Sagesse'.

These two songs, though not at all well known, are in many ways instructive; and it may be appropriate to use them as an excuse for dealing with an important point that frequently crops up in any critical examination of Stravinsky's output, namely, the question of poetic and musical subject matter.

As Paul Collaer rightly says, these two songs 'raise a question mark; they are enigmatic.' And from the standpoint of a French audience, 'they are upsetting.'

Whence comes this feeling of disquietude, since the musical value of these pieces is not in question? It is simply due to the fact that their quintessential character as music is at variance with the nature of Verlaine's poetical thought, which, far from being tethered to the literal sense of words or the palpable form of the ideas—which are mere accessories to poetry, though they are essentials to prose—is situated in a different atmosphere and operates on a different wave length. There is no doubt that the spirit of Verlaine's poetry was alien to a person of Stravinsky's thoroughly Slav mentality, even though he had a very thorough command of the French language. It was difficult for the musician to identify himself with the general ideas expressed in these two poems—the charm of moonlight; the despair of the soul confronted by its destiny—for such themes are only of universal application insofar as they can be treated as abstract ideas; but once they have passed through the prism of the poet's imagination they take on a special hue that gives them their unique poetic quality.

Although these two songs are not in the spirit of Verlaine, they have a musical idiom which is important in itself; and in order to appreciate it properly it is best to listen to them without the French text (or in the Russian translation, provided one is ignorant of that language). Distant though they may be from other more acceptable interpretations of the '*poète maudit*', they are of considerable interest from the standpoint of their musical content—especially the second in which appears one of the germinal motifs that was subsequently to haunt Stravinsky's mind and reappear in other of his compositions in many different guises. There is nothing here of the variegated shimmer of *The Fire Bird*. Instead, the music displays the hieratic seriousness of a Byzantine ikon that (by a strange but not inappropriate anachronism!) seems to emphasise the wisdom of Verlaine's repentance. This is the voice of Stravinsky the mystic, profoundly even fiercely religious, apparently ready to don sackcloth and even, if necessary, to embrace monastic austerity as a virtue.

BURLESQUE

'A puppet suddenly endowed with life, exasperating the patience of the orchestra with diabolical cascades of *arpeggi*, the orchestra in turn retaliating with menacing trumpet blasts, the outcome being a terrific noise which reaches its climax and ends in the sorrowful and querulous collapse of the poor puppet'*—such was the picture Stravinsky had in mind while writing a Konzertstück for piano and orchestra; and it came to him so unexpectedly, so spontaneously, that for the moment he did not altogether realise his good luck. This was the dramatic and musical kernel of what subsequently became, after a deliberate process of construction, the impulsive and truculent masterpiece known as *Petrushka*.

The score makes it clear that the main action of the ballet represents the Shrovetide Carnival that was held each year on the Admiralty Square, St. Petersburg, with its roundabouts, swings, sweetmeat stalls, toboggans, puppet theatres and all the other attractions of the fair. This forms the background to the drama of the poor little puppet who, tired of being continuously scoffed at and rebuffed by his sweetheart (the Ballerina), comes to blows with his rival, (the Moor), in an extraordinarily brief and unequal struggle, for Petrushka is unarmed and the Moor pursues him with a scimitar, as a result of which Petrushka collapses, shattered, and gives up his dislocated puppet soul.

As according to Stravinsky 'all music is nothing but a succession of impulses and repose'†, the composer's first preoccupation was to dis-

*Chronicle of My Life.

†*Poetics of Music* by Igor Stravinsky. Translated by Arthur Knodel and Ingolf Dahl. Harvard University Press, Cambridge, 1947.

cover which elements in his subject matter would provide esthetic justification for these two opposing principles.

In *Petrushka*, the crowd plays a part of considerable importance—in fact, it is the principal character and from the visual point of view owes its predominance to the picturesque costumes of people who had been drawn from every corner of Russia towards the capital, the centre at that time of all activities and all attractions. But it was also clear that this fantastic mixture of different types clad in different ways could not be directly rendered by music which, as Stravinsky has so rightly said,* 'does not and cannot have imitation for its object.' Did this mean that the crowd was nothing more than a picturesque kaleidoscope of costumes? That would have been a short-sighted view, for like individuals crowds have souls or—if one prefers—a psychological entity quick to react to outside stimulus and sensitive to every breath of wind. A crowd may be drifting along, aimlessly, thoughtlessly, almost at a standstill, emitting a vague kind of rumble; and suddenly something attracts its attention—an organ grinder, a bear-tamer, a group of nursemaids strolling by, each arm in arm with a coachman—and immediately the corporate mass reacts, all of them showing their interest and commenting on the event, and thereby regaining their own individual identities.

Here were two completely contrasted aspects of a corporate body like a crowd—the one static, the other mobile—aspects that a composer would be apt to translate into terms of 'impulses' and 'repose'.

There is no need to embark on a detailed analysis of the score in order to pin down one of the saliant characteristics of Stravinsky's invention: the deliberately calculating way in which, like an architect, he weighs up masses and volumes, balances materials by the cunning use of symmetry, uses polyphony to exploit the interplay of moments of stress and relaxation, and ultimately produces out of an extraordinarily heterogeneous collection of material a miraculous unity without which no work of art is valid. But architecture depends on the existence of certain materials; and in the case of *Petrushka* it was the Shrovetide Fair that, will-nilly, provided the subject matter of the ballet and the raw materials for the music. Stravinsky had to use his art to make musical sense of this material—allowing at one time a waltz ground out on a barrel-organ with some of its notes missing, or a commonplace flourish played on his flute by a showman, to rise above the general hurly-burly of the crowd. For the composer this might have been merely an agreeable technical problem to solve; but from the audience's point of view it could prove a matter of sheer delight—as when in the opening tableau a little waltz tune is combined with the air of *Ell' avait un' jamb' de bois* that was so popular in Paris during the years 1905-10, or when in the third tableau the Ballerina, after her gay, sentimental cornet-à-pistons solo, capriciously changes to a lively frivolous waltz (one of Lanner's *Danses Styriennes*) while the Moor tries clumsily to pay court to her. Translated

*Ibid.

into technical terms this meant the use of polyrhythm from the super-imposition of 3/4 on 2/4 and the simultaneous deployment of two different instrumental combinations: the one, shrill and sharp, the other heavy and low (in the style of a *Danse du ventre*), each with its appropriate percussion accompaniment.

It will be seen that, despite Stravinsky's affirmation that 'music is, by its very nature, essentially powerless to *express* anything at all, whether a feeling, an attitude of mind, a psychological mood or a phenomenon of nature'*, it can hardly be denied that there was a close link between the elements provided by the fair-ground and the composer's invention. And on scrutinising the work more closely it will be seen that this connection is even stronger because of the attitude adopted by Stravinsky to the purely dramatic part of the scenario, *viz.* the quarrel between the puppet and his rival. Had this drama been placed in the forefront of the action, the result would have been a new version of *I Pagliacci*, Leoncavallo's one-act realistic opera where there is abundance of pathos and little music. But the drama of Petrushka is no more than a single episode in the general tableau of the fair, though probably the most striking of all the various episodes that attract the attention of the crowd.

But who, indeed, are these characters who escape from the Showman's booth? Are they puppets, or live mountebanks who step out of their little theatre and mingle with the public in order to give a 'trailer' of the show? Nobody seems to know; and the crowd, which is at first amused though a trifle anxious, gradually becomes astonished and upset, until the moment when the Showman, who has been summoned by a policeman, shakes Petrushka's body and reveals it for what it is—a puppet figure stuffed with sawdust. So the drama was only a piece of horseplay after all; and the indifferent crowd melts away, while the sky grows dark and it begins to snow.

In this way, the ballet avoids the pitfalls of melodrama and romantic pathos and sentimentality; and by his treatment of the subject Stravinsky brings a new solution to the problem of musical spectacle at the same time as he fixes his musical style and idiom.

Petrushka has nothing in common with *The Fire Bird*. The earlier ballet sought to express oriental charm and succeeded in doing so with the help of an appropriate idiom and style of orchestration, using the refinements of chromaticism in a way that recalled the harmonic researches of the young French school. As opposed to the score of *The Fire Bird*, which is like a sumptuous many-coloured garment embroidered with gold, that of *Petrushka* reminds one of some kind of naive popular image. In it, Stravinsky repudiated charm and grace which until then had been looked on as essential musical qualities, and abjured the musical tradition inherited from the romantics. For him, neither the gesture of hand on the heart, nor that of head in the hands. But, as against this, he rehabilitated a quality which had hitherto been considered unworthy of

Chronicle of My Life.

great art, namely vulgarity. But let there be no misunderstanding, he subjected this quality to the demands of stylisation so that in becoming part of the whole it lost its pejorative aspect while preserving its popular spontaneity. In this way the popular tang of the accordeon, which in itself is hardly a very distinguished instrument, became one of the predominant features of the score so that it is no exaggeration to say that the whole work 'sounds as if it were written for a vast concertina.'* And it is the same with the roundabout music and the barrel-organ with its missing notes.

Here is another example of the close relationship between thought processes of Stravinsky and Picasso. In both cases one finds this double process of disarticulating natural elements in order to reach a new esthetic synthesis and of using material drawn from the pool of common experience, not by way of imitation or representation, but as a pretext for new musical or pictorial forms and developments. So music and painting may be said to progress hand in hand towards one of the main aims of contemporary esthetics: the independent life of a work of art divorced from its subject.

Translating this into technical terms, one might say that the medley of the fairground, with its music spreading all round and the puppets themselves, provided Stravinsky with a pretext for establishing an idiom divorced from traditional practice, built up by the superimposition of rhythms, harmonies and tonalities. The roots of these innovations could certainly be found in the works of the young French school, whose leading members had already overthrown old-fashioned dogmas and denounced academic prejudices. But henceforth Stravinsky was clearly a master in possession of new musical wealth and power—crude, audacious, paradoxical though it might be—and *Petrushka*, his first truly original work, perhaps did more than any other to contribute to his general popularity. The date of its first performance (13th June, 1911) deserves to rank as one of the great dates in the annals of contemporary music.

RIVALRY

While Stravinsky's star was definitely in the ascendant, another star was rising slowly above the horizon.

Although eight years older than his Russian contemporary, Arnold Schoenberg was at that time hardly known to the general public. The rare performances of his works, such as *Verklärte Nacht* at the Wiener Tonkünstlerverein in 1903 and *Pelleas und Melisande* at the Vereinigung Schaffender Tonkünstler in 1905, had at first met with indifference or lack of understanding. In 1907 the Kammersymphonie caused a scandal

Stravinsky by Paul Collaer. Brussels, 1930.

at its first performance in Vienna; and it was the same with the Quartet in F sharp minor when it was played the following year at the Bösendorfersaal. Despite these apparent setbacks, Schoenberg was recognised at this period as being a musician of considerable promise; and a number of devotees made no secret of their admiration. Among others, Gustav Mahler and a group of enthusiastic disciples including Alban Berg, Erwin Stein, Anton Webern and Egon Wellesz zealously followed his teaching and later became fervent exponents of his doctrines.

Self-taught like Stravinsky—but to an even greater extent—Schoenberg, unlike his Russian contemporary, had as a youth been an ardent Wagnerite and subsequently a great admirer of Brahms. Obsessed by an urge to explore the unknown, he had a natural penchant for the esoteric and resembled a strange alchemist bowed over his test-tubes in an attempt to isolate a priceless unknown element which he instinctively knew must exist. His first works were rather like the result of laboratory experiments undertaken originally with a view to enlarging the scope of what for centuries had served as the foundation of musical thought, namely, the system of tonality built up on the major and minor modes. But in the end these experiments led to the disruption of the old system.

It is true that in a work like *Tristan und Isolde* Wagner had considerably stretched the limitations of the classical system of tonality as practised by Rameau, Mozart and Beethoven—and even to some extent that of Schumann, Berlioz and Liszt. Nevertheless, those limitations still remained. All Schoenberg's efforts, seconded by his implacable will-power, were directed to the complete liberation of musical thought from its subjection to tonality; and he succeeded in his aim when in 1908 he wrote *Das Buch der Hängenden Gärten*, fifteen songs illustrating poems by Stefan George, the title of which seemed to have a symbolic meaning, for in this work he achieved a vague and suspended harmony, which later became known as atonality.

There has frequently been discussion about the possible influence of Schoenberg's music on Stravinsky during the years immediately preceding the first World War; and it is a fact that there are traces of it during the two years that separated *Petrushka* from *The Rite of Spring*. For instance, in the second of the Two Poems of Balmont entitled *The Dove*, there is a passage where a cluster of semitones packed tightly against each other within a restricted polyphonic space recalls the style of Schoenberg: but this is only a passing phase, for there is no trace of anything similar in the first of the Songs, *Blue Forget-me-not*, with its flavour of Ravel. It is rather *The King of the Stars*, a cantata for male choir and orchestra, that reveals a close relationship with the composer of *Erwartung*—to such an extent that Debussy, to whom it was dedicated, said a few years later in a letter to Robert Godet, 'Stravinsky is taking up a position dangerously close to that of Schoenberg.' Doubtless, Debussy, whose sensitive art was so closely related to the theory of intersensory correspondences as immortalised by Baudelaire in his well known reference to the interaction of 'perfumes, colours and sounds', looked on *The King of the Stars* as a work of complete abstraction.

But as both *The King of the Stars* and the Balmont Songs date from 1911, it is impossible to establish the slightest link between the traces of atonality they contain and *Pierrot Lunaire*, the first work of Schoenberg's that Stravinsky heard on the occasion of its performance on 8th December, 1912 at the Chorallon Saal, Berlin, and one which brought its composer sudden fame. This leads one to think that the moment of contact must have preceded this performance and been due to Stravinsky's familiarity with some of Schoenberg's printed music, unless the existence of these atonal passages can be explained as the result of Stravinsky's development of the chromatic processes used by Scriabin, whose symphonic poem *Prometheus* dates from 1910. But this latter supposition seems hardly credible in view of Stravinsky's almost physical aversion to the music of Scriabin; and the link with Schoenberg is infinitely more plausible since it is supported by fresh evidence subsequent to his acquaintance with *Pierrot Lunaire* supplied by the Three Japanese Lyrics written in 1913. *Tsaraiuki*, the third song in this delicate triptych, reveals one of the most characteristic aspects of Schoenberg's style with its wide leaping melodic intervals. This resemblance, however, is confined to the technical plane, and subsequent works showed little signs of it. For instance, the other two Japanese Lyrics, *Akahito* and *Masatzumi*, are closer to the style of *The Rite of Spring*, which was composed about the same time.

Schoenberg and Stravinsky were like two heavenly bodies that were sufficiently far apart for neither to affect the other's orbit. Nevertheless, from the moment of their meeting, each seems to have been somewhat distrustful of the other. After hearing *Pierrot Lunaire*, Stravinsky, while recognising 'the merits of the instrumentation',* showed no enthusiasm for a work which in his view was based on the aesthetic cult of Beardsley. This criticism is somewhat harsh and unjustified, for there is really not the slightest link between Schoenberg's esoteric art and chocolate-box pictures like *The Mysterious Rose Garden* or *The Toilet of Salome*. Furthermore, it is possible that traces of Beardsley may occasionally be found in some byway of Stravinsky's mind. It must be added that Schoenberg's attitude to Stravinsky was no less bitterly sarcastic. But it is best to ignore these sterile quarrels, for in the long run it is only the music that counts; and later on, further unexpected developments were to occur in the relationship between the two composers.

---

*Chronicle of My Life.

The Revolution of 'The Rite of Spring'

Diaghilev, Stravinsky and Prokofiev by Larionov

The Revolution of 'The Rite of Spring'

It is interesting to find that another vision—previous in fact to that of the poor puppet who leapt to fame as Petrushka—formed the genesis of *The Rite of Spring*. This time it was 'a solemn pagan rite'* which Stravinsky saw in his imagination during the spring of 1910 while finishing the last pages of *The Fire Bird*. This vision made so deep an impression on him that he described it immediately to his friend Nicholas Roerich, a painter who specialised in pagan subjects, and later to Diaghilev, who was at once carried away by the idea and determined to see the work brought to fruition. But he was much surprised later that summer, when visiting Stravinsky in Clarens, to be confronted by the contortions and imprecations of the future *Petrushka* instead of the sketches for the pagan symphonic poem he was expecting. As has already been explained, Diaghilev showed so much enthusiasm for the new ballet on Petrushka that for the moment the other project was shelved. In any case, Stravinsky realised that the composition of *The Rite of Spring* was bound to prove a long and difficult task;† and it was not until the summer of 1911, after he had drawn up the scenario with Roerich, that he was able to draft the first musical sketches.

*Chronicle of My Life.
†Ibid.

Les demoiselles d'Avignon, Picasso, 1907 (Museum of Modern Western Art, New York)

The scenario consists of a series of Tableaux of Pagan Russia divided into two parts: the first illustrating The Adoration of the Earth; the second, entitled The Sacrifice, expressing the primitive belief that death is a symbol of the renewal of life. From this episode in the biological cycle—the renaissance of the dormant forces hidden in the earth—the composer retained the dynamic impulse and used it as a motivating factor that animated all the components of his musical structure. So preponderant was the part played by rhythm that the first audiences that listened to *The Rite of Spring* found it was the only element they could immediately and spontaneously appreciate. Nevertheless, powerful though this rhythm may be, it would be a mistake to look on it as the only factor in *The Rite* and the sole source of the intense dynamic impulse generated by the work, for that is also due in no small measure to the special use of polyphony.

The principle already quoted in connection with *Petrushka*—that music consists of 'a succession of impulses and repose'—was adjusted here to an alternation of periods of stress and relaxation from which the composer obtained maximum effect thanks to a special use of poly-tonality. If polyphony is considered as a state of tonal equilibrium, it can be readily understood that the introduction into a musical structure in such a state of equilibrium of elements belonging to other distant tonalities will upset this stability, or at least set in motion its disruption, and from this anticipated but unachieved disruption is derived the feel-ing of extreme tension to be found in certain passages of *The Rite*. It is as if a wedge were being driven into a piece of wood until it is on the point of splitting.

From the aesthetic point of view, this polytonal procedure, when handled by a master (as is the case here) produces an effect of tremendous power; but the resultant sonorities were so novel that they were bound at a first hearing to disconcert an unprepared audience. Some—indeed, the majority—found it a brutal transition to pass from the blandish-ments of *Le Jongleur de Notre Dame* or *Roma* (first performed in 1912) to this cataclysm of sound that resembled an earthquake.

As for the handful of music-lovers who were seriously interested in new music, they expected something quite different from a composer who had created a glittering oriental fairy-tale in *The Fire Bird* and a picturesque piece of clowning in *Petrushka*. And it should also be re-membered that the brilliant renaissance of the French school led by Debussy and Ravel had as its watchword the need for extreme subtlety, and here the magic of orchestral colouring played a predominant part.

The reaction was violent. The uproar at the first performance was so great that after a short time it was impossible to hear the music, and the blows that broke out between the supporters and opponents of the work suddenly turned the Théâtre des Champs-Elysées, of which this was the inaugural season, into a ringside arena. Stravinsky no longer had any need to feel envious of Schoenberg: the Parisian scandal of *The Rite*

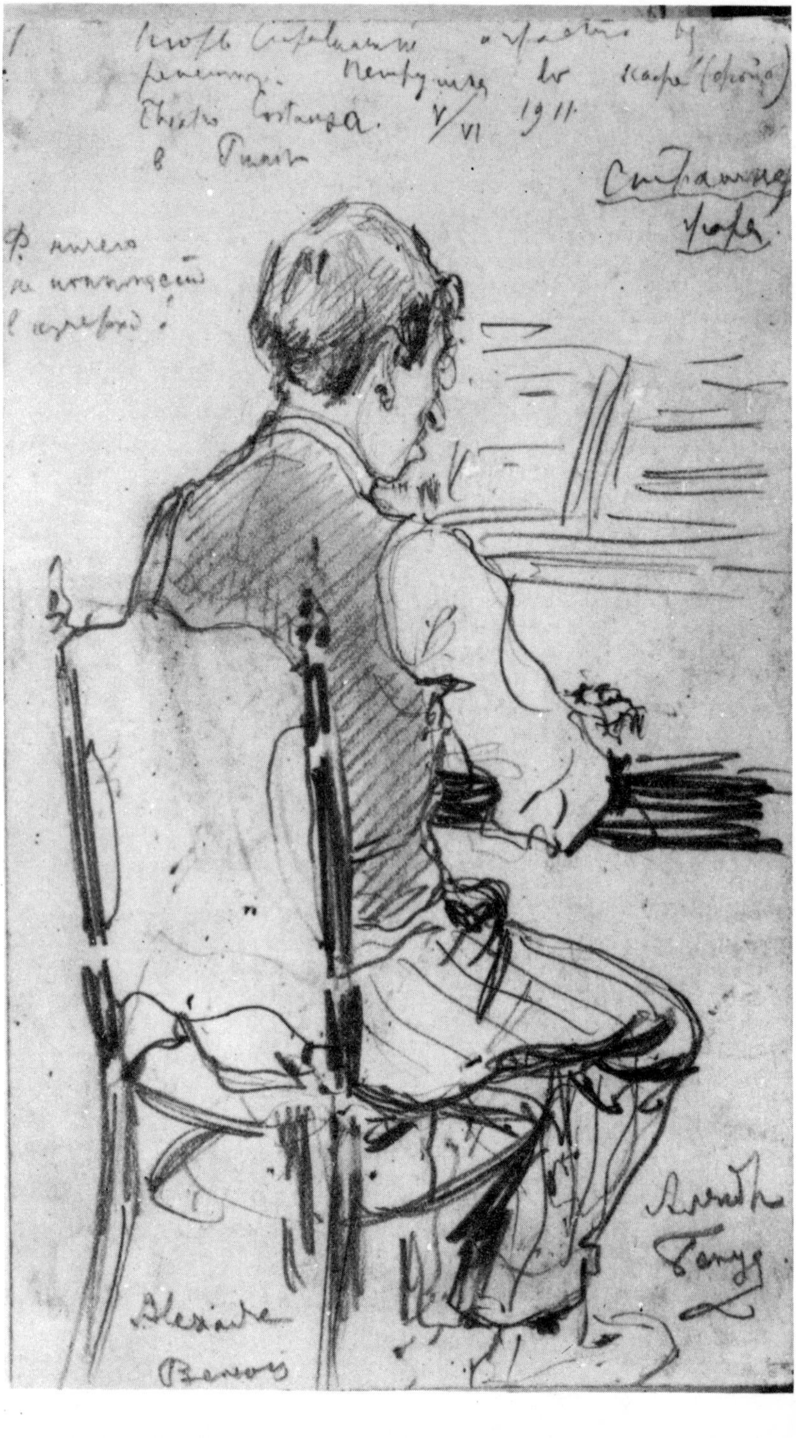
V/VI 1911
Alexandre
Benois

of Spring was a worthy counterpart to the Viennese scandal of the Kammersymphonie, and also to the outcry in artistic circles that had been created six years earlier by Picasso's painting of *Les Demoiselles d'Avignon*.

The critics, though divided in their opinions of the work, were unanimous in disapproving of the attitude of the public. From that date (29th May, 1913) two groups were formed, two hostile parties that pursued their squabbles both privately and in the public press—the one side feeling themselves outraged and looking on *The Rite* as the negation of all that music stood for, the other side hailing it as the dawn of a new era. Once again it was Alfred Bruneau who showed himself the most perceptive critic of the new work and had the courage immediately after the première to call it a 'daring musical synthesis'. Though more reticent in the expression of his views, Louis Vuillemin prophesied that 'time would show its true worth'.

We are now in a better position to judge. Today no sincere critic would dare to deny that *The Rite* is a magnificent success in the sense that the musical means employed are absolutely compatible with the basic scenario and its startlingly primitive character, and with the mysterious power of the renewal of life that made so deep an impression on primitive man, and which in Northern Russia, with its long winter nights, brings about the liberation of earth and water from their frozen bondage.

It was the most natural thing in the world that this musical evocation should have the effect of a revolution. But Stravinsky has protested violently against the suggestion that his music for *The Rite* is 'revolutionary'—and rightly so if the word is used in its pejorative sense of 'disorderly'. But if (as Stravinsky says)★ 'A musical complex, however harsh it may be, is legitimate to the extent to which it is genuine', one can maintain that 'revolution' may also mean the installation of a new order. And in this sense *The Rite* is certainly a revolutionary work, though it must be recognised that it is 'revolutionary' in quite a different way from the atonal music of Schoenberg or Webern, for what it sets out to do is not so much to suspend or destroy tonality as to enlarge its range and intensify its power. Technical analysis shows that, contrary to first impressions, it is based on the same sort of harmonic foundation as works of the classical period, so that it is difficult to tell whether it is really a culmination or a point of departure, a prolongation of tradition or a break with the past.

In any case, there is no doubt that the formal structure of the component parts, completely differs from classical procedure in view of Stravinsky's special attitude to time and metre. Not only does his metrical treatment lead to new rhythms, but it also affects the line of melodic development, which shows its Slav origins by the use of reiterated patterns that form the basis of oriental ornamentation.

★*Poetics of Music.*

AU THÉÂTRE DES CHAMPS-ÉLYSÉES

"Le Sacre du Printemps"
Ballet en deux actes, de M. Igor Stravinsky

— Où donc ont-ils été élevés tous ces salauds-là ?

Telle est la phrase la plus conciliante qui fut proférée parmi tant d'autres au cours de cette soirée élégante et mémorable.

Elle résume à elle seule la stupeur que l'on doit éprouver en constatant la méchanceté stupide et raisonnée de ce qu'on est convenu d'appeler l'élite parisienne, en présence de toute tentative véritablement neuve et hardie. Ce même public qui, depuis des années, ne proteste pas contre les plus plats vaudevilles, contre les restes d'opérettes accommodés à la sauce anglaise qu'on lui offre chaque jour, ce public surtout qui voit, quotidiennement ce qu'il y a de plus laid au point de vue plastique et qui entend ce que l'on dit de plus bête, puisqu'il achète des miroirs et qu'il le reçoit, ce même public affecte une souffrance intolérable lorsqu'un artiste, épris d'étrangeté, essaie de lui faire entrevoir une conception neuve, de l'amuser ou de l'intéresser par des lignes et des mouvements jusqu'alors inconnus.

Le vrai snobisme, depuis Thackeray, est fait, quoi qu'on en pense, de réaction et non de hardiesse. Il n'admet que de vieilles audaces cent fois éprouvées et admises par une caste. L'audace véritable appartient aux seuls artistes. C'est donc avec respect et attention que l'on a admiré pour la centième fois, Les Danses du Prince Igor, puisque leurs naïvetés primitives sont photographiées dans les manuels d'histoire et de géographie, c'est avec horreur que l'on a accueilli Le Sacre du Printemps, parce qu'il s'agissait de mettre en scène des mœurs plus anciennes, antérieures aux manuels d'histoire à l'usage des gens du monde. Il est vrai que la plupart des spectateurs présents n'ont pas dû comprendre le titre. Les hommes ont dû croire qu'il s'agissait d'injures et les femmes de modes nouvelles lancées par un magasin de nouveautés.

Ce fut donc, en tendant l'oreille, au milieu d'un chahut indescriptible qu'il nous fallut, péniblement, nous faire une idée approximative de l'œuvre nouvelle, également empêchés de l'entendre par ses défenseurs et ses adversaires. On respecte jusqu'au bout les droits de la défense en cour d'assises; des artistes qui ont fait leurs preuves n'ont point droit, au théâtre, aux mêmes égards. Cela donne envie de se faire apache.

Tout ceci ne signifie point, je me hâte de le dire, que cette œuvre nouvelle soit à l'abri de toute critique. Loin de là. Les auteurs et les interprètes ont réalisé un invraisemblable tour de force en mettant à la scène, durant deux actes, les gestes primitifs, inconscients, puérils, frénétiques de peuplades primitives, s'éveillant aux mystères de la vie, mais l'œuvre d'art, je le faisais observer dernièrement encore, ne saurait être fondée uniquement sur le grossier ou sur le laid. Quelle que soit, par exemple, en France, notre curiosité ethnographique pour les monuments druidiques, nous ne saurions décemment en adopter le style décoratif dans notre vie privée ; l'art munichois de l'ameublement peut seul concevoir de telles erreurs. Si l'on utilise la laideur dans l'art, ce ne peut être que comme terme de comparaison. Rien ne s'opposait, par exemple, à ce que l'on nous offrît, dans Le Sacre du Printemps, les gestes inférieurs de peuplades primitives à condition que cette expression fût brève, accessoire, et ne remplît pas deux actes.

C'est la tort de tous les artistes qui découvrent une idée nouvelle, de ne pouvoir suffisamment, tout d'abord, la synthétiser. Leur petite découverte, si géniale qu'elle soit, est toujours exposée avec trop de complaisance. C'est le grand avantage des idées polies par le temps que de s'exprimer au contraire avec élégance et brièveté. Quelques gestes amusants, nouveaux, justes, suffisent à évoquer des peuplades barbares; il est inutile de les répéter trop longuement.

Il faut enfin, je le répète, que l'artiste, un peu à la manière des romantiques, nous propose toujours la beauté à côté de la laideur. Une intervention personnelle de Nijinsky eût suffi peut-être pour remettre au point Le Sacre du Printemps; peut-être aussi une évocation plastique de la nature, qui était aussi belle jadis qu'aujourd'hui,

Mlle PILTZ (La Jeune Fille)   Photo Gerschel

If at this point one reconsiders the doctrine of the divorce of music from expression as enunciated by Stravinsky himself, it will be seen that everything in *The Rite of Spring* contradicts it. To begin with, the music is the perfect partner of the spectacle it sets out to illustrate. And then, whatever may be said to the contrary, there was the initial vision of 'sage elders, seated in a circle, watching a young girl dance herself to death'* which was the genesis of this extraordinary work. Furthermore, during the year or more that it was being composed, other images of one kind or another are very likely to have passed through the composer's mind.

Whereas to some persons the creator of *The Rite* appeared like a threatening figure of Moloch ready to crunch up in his formidable jaws and devour the musical standards hitherto based on the representation of beauty, to others he became the infallible prophet of a new aesthetic. As a result of *The Rite* Stravinsky found himself regarded as a portent in the musical world, and there were times later on in his career when he could hardly recognise the figure of himself that had been built up in the imagination of the public.

THE NIGHTINGALE

A few days after the tumultuous première of *The Rite of Spring*, Stravinsky succumbed to an attack of typhoid fever and was incapacitated for several weeks. The solicitude shown by his Parisian friends gave him a chance of realising how deep was the interest and affection he had aroused. The main figures of the musical life of Paris—de Falla, Ravel, Casella, Florent Schmitt, Debussy—all visited his sickbed; and Diaghilev and Maurice Delage called at his nursing home almost every day.

Back at Ustilug, he still felt rather weak, so he confined himself to writing 'several small little things', †including the Three Little Songs (Memories of his Childhood) that have already been mentioned above. But on his return to Clarens in Switzerland where he had decided to spend the winter, he received a proposal from the newly founded Free Theatre of Moscow, which caused him considerable embarrassment—this was a request for his opera *The Nightingale*, the composition of which had been interrupted, when only the first of three acts had been completed, by the commission to write *The Fire Bird*. By the time he pulled it out of his drawer and looked once again at the faded pages, over four years had elapsed, during which he had made tremendous technical strides as a composer and opened up many new musical vistas. The question was—should he now attempt to rewrite the first act with its manifest echoes of Debussy and Rimsky-Korsakov? Perhaps it would have been wiser to do so. Nevertheless, it is extremely difficult com-

Chronicle of My Life.
†*Ibid.*

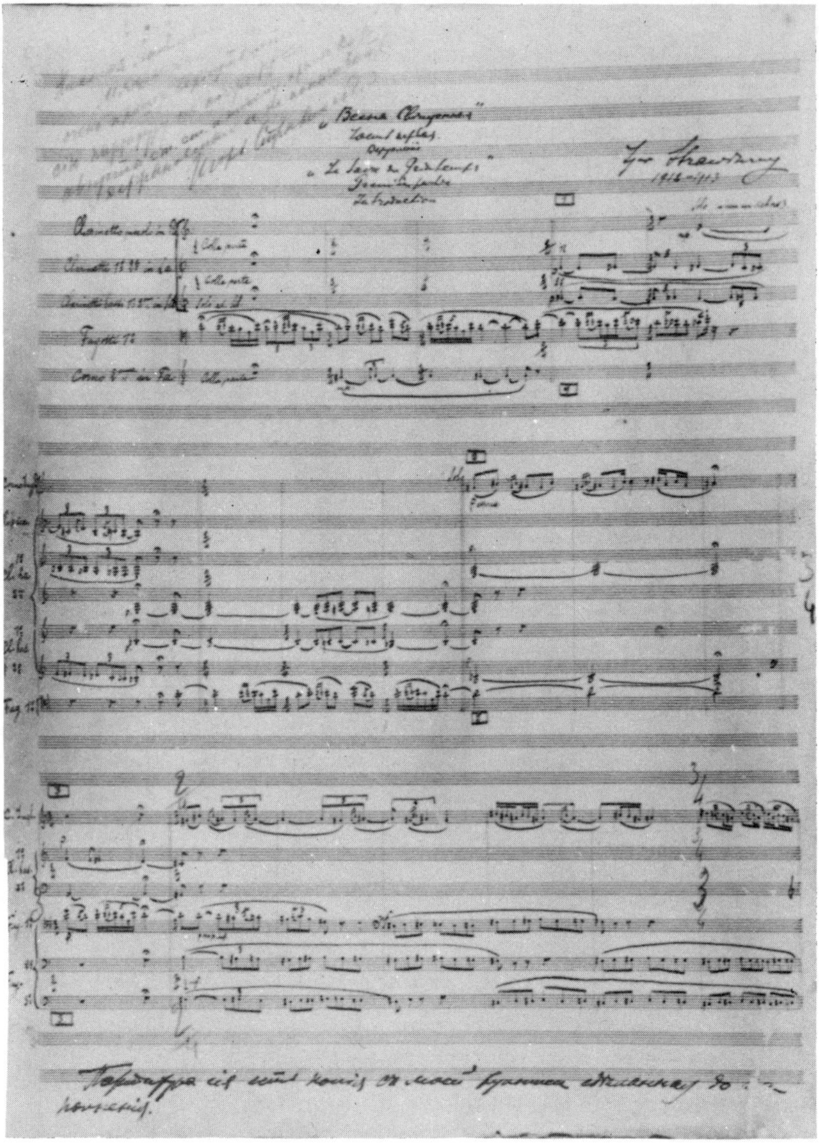

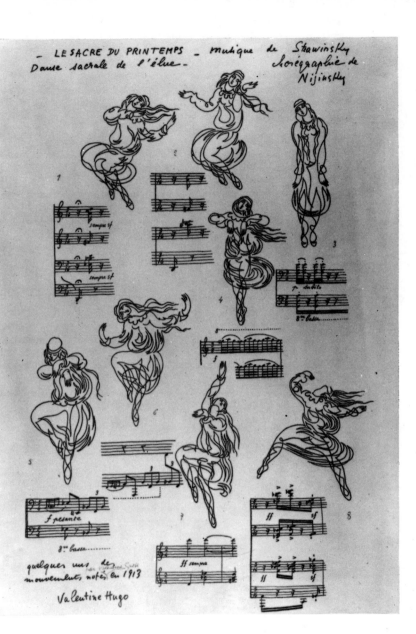

pletely to rewrite a composition once it has already been drafted. Nor was it feasible for him to continue Acts II and III in the style of the first act.

But this was not the only difficulty to be solved. In addition, there was the question of the opera's musical form. At various times in his career Stravinsky was to try out a number of different solutions to this problem in his reaction against Wagnerian music drama with its principle of 'endless melody' which he was later to stigmatise as 'the perpetual becoming of a music that never had any reason for starting, any more than it had any reason for ending'.* It was accordingly natural that he should incline towards the ancient operatic forms with their clear contours and the symmetry of their airs and ensembles. In dealing with the libretto, he favoured a light touch of clowning rather than treating it as serious drama; and in the opera the effect is so delicately sketched that it appears like a scarcely perceptible ironic smile playing lightly over the lips of the teller of this fairy tale from the Far East.

Naturally the dynamic harshness of a work like *The Rite of Spring* would have been out of place here. The artificial magnificence and glitter of the Imperial Court of the imaginary Kingdom of China were sufficient excuse for Stravinsky to construct various shimmering sound effects based on the exotic black-note or pentatonic scale. In doing so, he doubtless remembered the *Pagodes* of Debussy and Ravel, and added his own special brand of polytonality. But it should not be forgotten that others had anticipated him in the use of this device, for in the final dance of *Daphnis et Chloé* (finished in 1911, though the early sketches went back as far as 1909) Ravel had already succeeded in splitting the polyphonic structure so that different tonalities could develop independently on different levels. One should also remember the strange harmonic agglomerations occurring in the *Habanera* (1895) that Ravel wrote at the age of 23 and which was later incorporated in his *Rhapsodie Espagnole*.

In trying to relate *The Nightingale* to the rest of Stravinsky's output, recent critics have pointed out that this opera is usually considered to be a bastard production. It is true that the technical unity established between the three acts by the repeated song of the fisherman, which forms a framework for the opera, and by the use of thematic motifs (somewhat on Wagnerian lines) does not succeed in producing a truly unified style. To achieve such a unity, one needs more than the artificial deployment of material links. As Delacroix said, 'Style is the equilibrium of impulse and form'.†

And Stravinsky himself must have felt this too, for in 1917 he agreed to a suggestion from Ernest Ansermet, the conductor of the Orchestre de la Suisse Romande, that he should condense the opera into a symphonic poem. The first act, which lay outside the impulse that had led

*Poetics of Music.
† Diary, by Eugène Delacroix.

50

Alexandre Benois and Stravinsky, 1911

to the composition of the rest of the work, was then simply eliminated.

The original stage version of the opera saw the light of day, not in Moscow where the Free Theatre enterprise had met a sudden and untimely end, but in Paris where Diaghilev mounted it in the course of his 1914 season at the Opéra. It was given in the same bill as Rimsky-Korsakov's *Golden Cockerel*, with whose chromatic vocalisation it has points of close resemblance.

After Diaghilev's Paris season, Stravinsky wrote Three Pieces for

String Quartet at Salvan in the Valais, which can be looked on as experiments in sound. It is certainly curious that they should coincide with similar experiments that were being made by Schoenberg at the same time. They are a new by-product of the tendency towards abstraction already revealed in his cantata *The King of the Stars*.

At this moment Stravinsky undertook a journey, which in the light of after-events was to assume a special significance. After a brief stay at Ustilug, he went on to Kiev before making the return journey to Switzerland where he had planned to spend the summer. Why did he make this detour? Kiev, situated on the Dnieper, is (like Novgorod) one of the oldest towns in Russia. In the second half of the ninth century, the Vareg Oleg made it the capital of his kingdom. In 957 it was the scene of Princess Olga's conversion to Christianity, and this led in 988 to the baptism of her son Vladimir and the attachment of Russia—hitherto a pagan country—to the Greek Orthodox Church. Between the eleventh and twelfth centuries it became the capital of all Russia. Small wonder that it has since become the depository of many precious documents; and it was here that Stravinsky laid hands on various collections of Russian folklore, of which he made a comprehensive selection for future use.

But the storm clouds were piling up on every side. On his return journey to Switzerland via Warsaw, Berlin and Basle, he could feel the temperature of Europe rising; and barely a fortnight after he had got back to Clarens, the first World War broke out.

REFUGE IN THE VAUD

The outbreak of the War brought the first part of Stravinsky's musical career to a close. The Paris of the *belle époque* had passed away, never to return, and indeed the glories of that golden age were almost completely forgotten in the Paris of the post-war period. At the age of thirty-two, he had already created a number of key-works, including *Fireworks*, *The Fire Bird*, *Petrushka* and *The Rite of Spring*. These compositions, where oriental magic was joined with popular clowning, where mysterious and fascinating legends rubbed shoulders with uncouth primitive customs, were animated by an extraordinary dynamic quality that revealed itself in the preponderant rhythmic impulse of the music. In comparison with such rich profusion and vitality, other groups of his works appear less spontaneous, even austere. Nevertheless, there is no gainsaying that the harsh hieratic quality of the Verlaine Poems and the bare abstractions of *The King of the Stars* and the Three Pieces for String Quartet are just as characteristic of Stravinsky's mind, which while it was being pushed in one direction by Dionysiac forces of inspiration, was being pulled in another by the Apollonian will to control and

Portrait of Stravinsky, Gleize, 1914

Portrait
de RAMUZ
par
J Stravy
29 Juin 1917
chez Noverraz
Lausanne

discipline such forces in favour of pure reason. But the most remarkable thing of all is the unity that binds together these two opposing tendencies: a special way of thinking that bears the mark of Stravinsky's Slav origins.

Meanwhile, the shadow of the war spread over the whole of Western Europe; and even the neutral countries, though managing to keep aloof from the conflict, suffered much inconvenience, and even misery. Surrounded on all sides by belligerents, Switzerland found herself in a particularly difficult situation. After a year or two, the householders who were suffering from a rash of wartime restrictions began to dig up their lawns and flower-beds and convert them into kitchen gardens. Even the countryside was affected, and most of the arable land was turned over to wheat and potatoes. Postal communication with foreign countries became so difficult that it more or less ceased and those who were resident in Switzerland gradually succumbed to a vague and miserable sensation that they were living in a vacuum, isolated from the mad hurly-burly of the world at war outside.

It is easy to imagine Stravinsky's feelings as, cut off from the comforts of his country estate at Ustilug, the excitements of the theatre and the attractions of smart society, he found himself living in quiet rural seclusion in the Canton of Vaud, where during the next four years he was to move from Clarens to Salvan, from Morges to Les Diablerets

Stravinsky, Madame K., Diaghilev and Bakst, Lausanne, 1915

and the Chateau d'Oex, then back to Morges again, continually on the lookout for a suitable spot where he and his family could settle down. And all the time his mind was filled with an intense longing for his native land. This helps to explain his special fondness at that moment for the popular verses he had brought out of Russia just before the outbreak of the War, like a treasure saved from a holocaust. He read them over and over again, and enjoyed not only their truculence, but also their unexpected metaphors, the characteristic cadences and sounds formed by the words and phrases, by the play of syllables against each other, which reminded him of analogous procedures in the business of musical composition and doubtless brought him a nostalgic whiff of his native land. Sometimes these verses were no more than onomatopoeic rhymes, of no greater significance than the popular jingles with simple assonances and well marked rhythms that are used by boys and girls all the world over. While other verses might contain a mixture of roguishness and fantasy, their real appeal was as direct as a sudden nudge or wink or smile, and their racy quality seemed to call for a certain polyphonic crudity in their setting, traces of which could be found in some of Stravinsky's earlier works. The *Pribaoutki* songs mark a new stage; and the composer seems to have abandoned the faded oriental pageantry of *The Nightingale* for the lively colours of peasant embroidery and the sort of toys and trinkets that are peddled round Russian villages.

> *Come on, dear Uncle Kornilo,*
> *Harness your mare;*
> *And at Makara's on the sand,*
> *Drive away your worries.**

The lazy working tune swings between two short melodic phrases that are repeated with slight variations. The eight instruments (string quartet plus woodwind quartet) seem determined to confuse the issue by disguising the simple diatonic character of the vocal line with polytonal accompaniment of considerable subtlety despite its apparent crudity. But suddenly there is an outburst of laughter:—

> *Home-brewed ale stands in a jug—*
> *Intoxicating strong ale;*
> *Jovial is the intoxicated head;*
> *Drink up, drink to the dregs.*

The music seems to dance like sunlight caught in the glass of ale, and the song ends with a cadence from oboe and clarinet that sounds like a prolonged chuckle. It is almost as if one were present at one of the

*These and the subsequent translations from the Russian of the *Pribaoutki* songs are by Sarah S. White.

sessions that Stravinsky and Ramuz used to enjoy at La Crochettaz when they called for a portion of good cheese and washed it down with a half litre of Dézaley.

The friendship of the Swiss writer Ramuz was a godsend to Stravinsky during these years of exile in the Vaud. As a man of letters Ramuz was devoted to his native tongue, the language of the Suisse Romande; and this was well suited to express the popular raciness of Stravinsky's Russian folk texts. Not only did Ramuz provide an incomparable translation of these works, but he also became a close friend of Stravinsky's sharing with him the difficulties, anxieties and bitter disappointments of those wartime years.

Meanwhile, this collaboration which was to prove so fruitful in the course of the next four years had produced its first fruits in Ramuz's translation of the text of the four *Pribaoutki* poems: *Uncle Armand* (which has already been mentioned); *The Oven* where a cook is busy baking in the kitchen, while outside

> *The ducks begin to play their pipes*
> *And the cranes begin to dance;*

The Colonel, who

> *. . . set off for a walk*
> *And caught a small quail.*
> *The quail wanted to drink:*
> *So she flew up, fluttered,*
> *Found herself under the ice*
> *And caught a priest—*
> *Pop Popovitch—*
> *Peter Petrovitch;*

and finally the somewhat enigmatic fable of *The Old Man and The Hare*.

In addition to their earthy savour, these musical jokes are of special interest since they served as a try-out for one of Stravinsky's most important works, perhaps his masterpiece. The composition of *The Wedding (Les Noces)*, originally entitled *The Village Wedding*, was spread over a long period, since the cantata begun in July 1914 only received its definite instrumentation nine years later in April 1923. Nevertheless, the short score was finished by 1917: so the work can properly be said to belong to Stravinsky's Vaudois period and like the other compositions he wrote at this time reveals the fact that during the first three years of the War he was mainly preoccupied with thoughts and images of his native land.

Design by Goncharova for 'The Wedding'

A BOUQUET OF SONGS

The subject of *The Wedding* is a simple one: it is entirely concerned with the busy preparations for a village marriage and (as epilogue) the traditional scene of junketing. It is like a tableau by Teniers—or, rather, Hieronymus Bosch—transposed to an Ukrainian *isba*, where the main parts are played by characters from Russian peasant life—on the one hand, the bride and groom with their parents and relations; on the other, the crowd of uncles, aunts, cousins, friends and neighbours drawn together from the surrounding countryside and attracted by the prospect of the festivities and the good fare.

There are four tableaux. In the first ('The Tress') the young girls of the village are chattering round Timofeevna, dressing her hair and preparing her for the ceremony. The second ('The Groom') is a pendant to the first. The third ('Departure of the Bride') is a very brief invocation to the Virgin and the Saints, suggesting the wedding ceremony without directly portraying it. The fourth ('The Wedding Breakfast'), is the most developed of the four and as lively and quarrelsome as could be wished.

The action is twofold in the sense that part of it is concerned with the excitement of the crowd happily preoccupied with games, jokes, food and all the animal pleasures of the feast, while the other part deals with the gravity of the married couple's vows—particularly those of Timofeevna, who resembles the Chosen Victim of *The Rite of Spring* and, like her is offered up as a sacrifice, not to the rebirth of spring, but to life and the unknown sorrows that may be in store for her. There is no question of love in this union that has been negotiated between the two families. *Cad!* cries one of the guests during the wedding breakfast, *you've sold your daughter for a glass of wine!* Doubtless one should allow for a drunkard's pardonable exaggeration: but the remark is typical of the atmosphere of this particular wedding.

And the sadness of the married couple's farewell to their past, which after all was a happy time now irretrievably lost, falls like a passing shadow on this tableau of noisy gaiety, and is as poignant as the comparable passage in *Petrushka* where the puppet hero appears to die. There is perhaps no more quietly moving moment than the scene at the end of *The Wedding* where after the bedroom door has been closed on the married couple, the bride's father, suddenly realising the gap made in his family, remains alone on the stage to express his deep sadness, while all around him, after the conclusion of the wedding festivities, bells peal and die away into silence.

It is at this point that Stravinsky reveals himself as not only an architect of sound but also a dramatist. The father's bass solo is balanced by another solo: the lament of Timofeevna with which the score opens. This is not due merely to a feeling for symmetry, for the hearing of the score makes it clear that the drama of the main protagonists imparts a special dramatic significance to the various picturesque scenes and imposes a sense of unity which pervades the whole work.

The Wedding is a strange work, which seems to escape formal classification. It is true that at first, in conformity with the score's subtitle, it was presented as a suite of choreographic scenes. But it is clear that in Stravinsky's mind the music was something different from a ballet score. The visual images that may have inspired the subject had no specifically choreographic implications; and Nijinska's admirable scenic adaptation owed its success to its deliberate rejection of all realism. At the basis of the conception of *The Wedding* there is nothing comparable to the visions that were the genesis of *The Rite* and *Petrushka*, nor to the narrative quality implicit in the scenarios of *The Fire Bird* and *The Nightingale*. The new score, though apparently intended for stage performance, seemed to mark a change of direction in the composer's mind; and the fact that it is based solely on the development of musical material puts it at once in the category of 'pure music'.

On the other hand, it may be objected that it has a text and is accordingly related to a literary subject. But there is every indication that the text is there merely to support the voices, and for the greater part of the time it has no logical meaning at all. Moreover, the way the vocal parts are interwoven makes it clear that the composer was not in the least concerned to make this text intelligible to his audience.

In that case, how can one possibly pretend (as in fact has frequently been done) that *The Wedding* is a cantata or an oratorio? In those musical forms, it is impossible to neglect the sense of the words, since their function is to set forth the dramatic or psychological lines of action at the same time as the more or less stylised expression of various sentiments or states of mind of the main characters. Moreover, a cantata or oratorio is usually divided into separate numbers separated from each other by pauses or recitatives, airs, duets, ensembles, which remind one of the wings of an altar-piece where each separate picture is complete within its own frame.

There is nothing like that in *The Wedding*, where the four scenes follow without pause with a continuous stream of melodies that go on renewing themselves until the last pages of the score. This is a long way from the concision of classicism and the conception of economy of means that John Sebastian Bach, the great master of cantata and fugue, erected into so rigid a system that in his view the two-theme sonata was incompatible with the exigencies of the law of unity.

The multiplicity of melodic themes that enter into the composition of *The Wedding* would remind one of a *pot-pourri*, were it not for the fact that such an image implies a measure of disorder, and this is abolutely uncharacteristic of the score.

If, instead of concentrating on the forty themes or more that proliferate in this musical fresco, one turns to examine the rhythm, the presence of Bach is immediately felt—particularly the unflagging energy that motivates the Brandenburg Concertos. By taking the shortest syllable as his unit, i.e. the quaver, Stravinsky like Bach succeeds in relating his various melodic themes to a common denominator; and the score of *The Wedding* then reveals itself in its most simple and accessible aspect as a series of variations on a single rhythmic principle— a regular beat like the movement of a well-regulated watch.

But apart from this metronomical unity, there seems to be no other point of contact with Bach, for all these short syllables, these quavers— or, if one prefers the simile, the ticking of the watch—are not grouped in uniform bars as in classical music where common time is related to the march or certain dance forms, triple time to the stately minuet, the vivacious scherzo, or the light-footed waltz. Instead, the incessant chatter of these short syllables forms a solid chunk which divides up into bars of various lengths and different time signatures, and makes the conductor's task a particularly hazardous one. These different rhythms are superimposed on each other, echo each other, and intertwine between the parts of the chorus, the soloists, and the accompanying orchestra of four pianos, which call for four virtuoso pianists, and a big percussion section. The result is a polyphonic score of surpassing

Listening to Stravinsky, Hanich, 1956

richness, which makes use of all the new resources opened up by poly-tonality and polyrhythm, which might have been invented on purpose to depict the picturesque hurly-burly of this particular fete.

A bouquet of songs—that is a proper description of *The Wedding*—a bunch of country flowers arranged with consummate art; a profusion of songs, with no apparent links between one and the other, thrown together in confusion for no apparent reason, or for the pure pleasure (sometimes a little trivial) of giving someone a couplet when he's raising his glass in the midst of the rather coarse jokes of the assembled company.

The Chorale reflected the unquestioning piety of a composer like J. S. Bach; the Lied was the ideal vehicle for expressing the romanticism of a Weber or Schumann. In his turn, Stravinsky, dreaming of his native land, produced song after song from Russian folk lore, extracted from the rich treasure he had brought back to Switzerland from the Ukraine just before the outbreak of the War. Indeed, such a strong family feeling unites these songs, with their ability to evoke a previous age, that it is difficult to tell which of them are authentic folksongs and which are Stravinsky's own compositions. In their robust vigour they seem to recall an ancient Russia, still at the dawn of Christianity, perhaps even before the age of Jenghiz Khan: some very primitive ones are built up on no more than three or four notes; others are formed out of archaic scales, closely related to the plainsong of Western Europe, which reached Russia from Greece through Byzantium.

The pure line of these melodies—like the line drawings of faces and arabesques to be found on the sides of ancient vases—may be derived from the fact that like these vase designs they too ignore the discipline of perspective—and by that I mean the laws of harmony, which while pretending to offer a logical system for the composition of music, have merely succeeded in placing within the reach of composers without a shred of talent a mass of platitudes and clichés that become rapidly worn out because they are completely empty of invention. The same mistake, in the realm of sound, can be observed in the visual arts during periods of academic stagnation, when the primary aesthetic aim becomes the slavish imitation of approved models.

It is in that direction that the real value of *The Wedding* lies. More so perhaps than any of Stravinsky's previous works, this composition shows that it benefitted from the lesson formulated by the paintings of Cézanne and Picasso; it denies itself the luxury of representation and achieves solely through the use of objective musical forms the sort of meta-morphosis caused by the transfiguration of realism. And it is in this sense too that, though built up only of songs, it can be said to form one of the great masterpieces of pure sound. Furthermore, with its profusion of thematic and rhythmic material, and the wealth of its new and daring polyphonic combinations, it contains the germ of an idea which was to be more clearly expressed in some of the composer's later works.

Juan Gris, 1917 (Louise Leiris Gallery)

It is a score rich in promise, a music literally illustrating Stravinsky's characteristic appetite for creation, which at that period of his exile was particularly strong. As he was to say some years later, *'we have a duty towards music, namely to invent it'*.★

★*Poetics of Music.*

Diaghilev: Russian caricature, 1909

ROME AND PARIS

Not unnaturally there were occasions when Stravinsky felt it necessary to leave this rarefied atmosphere and descend from the heights. He did this on two planes—by refreshing himself with the composition of less strenuous works than *The Wedding* and by abandoning the isolation of neutral Switzerland for an occasional trip abroad. These difficult wartime journeys were usually undertaken at the instigation of Diaghilev. On one of them Stravinsky visited Rome for the first time in the winter of 1915-16, and this was the occasion of a rather amusing incident connected with his liking for musical jokes.

As soon as he met Diaghilev, he took out of his bag the manuscript of Three Easy Pieces which he had recently written for piano duet. Doubtless these were intended for his son, Soulima, since the bass in each piece was a simple and unchanging formula—a chord spread over two quavers in the March, two bars of accompaniment in the Waltz, and four quavers in the Polka—while the more skilled player in the treble carried out a series of amusing variations above these ostinatos with their simple and familiar rhythms.

The two men sat down at the piano, Stravinsky playing the treble, Diaghilev the bass. Each piece carried a dedication: the March was for Alfredo Casella, the Waltz for Erik Satie, the Polka for Diaghilev. When they reached the third piece Stravinsky explained that in composing it he had thought of Diaghilev as a circus ringmaster in evening dress and top-hat, cracking his whip and urging on a rider—something like a sketch by Toulouse-Lautrec, unless perhaps he was thinking of Seurat's painting of The Circus. At first Diaghilev was nonplussed and seemed about to take offence; but in the end he realised that behind his friend's pretended seriousness there was a twinkle in his eye, and the two men had a good laugh over the musical joke, despite the other worries that preoccupied them.

Indeed, business affairs were not going very well for either of them at that particular moment. Stravinsky had had to incur fairly heavy expenses in repatriating his mother at a moment when his own income from his Russian property reached him only with difficulty and hardly sufficed to meet the needs of his family, which consisted of his wife, who was in delicate health, and four children, Theodore, Ludmila, Soulima and Milene.

As for Diaghilev, his company was scattered about Europe owing to the exigencies of the War, and this meant that he was prevented from exercising his natural function as an impresario. He too was cut off from his native country and, despite his ostentatious mode of living, had no other means of livelihood than that provided by the Russian Ballet. Any less pertinacious person would have been discouraged by the innumerable obstacles that had to be overcome before his company could be reformed. Nijinsky and his wife had to be freed from the concentration camp in Hungary where they had been interned; and all the scenery and costumes and other material had to be reassembled for a projected tour of the United States. Nevertheless, by dint of force and skill, Diaghilev succeeded and as a prelude to this Atlantic voyage organised two festival performances of music and dance: the first on 20th December, 1915, at Geneva, where the ballet company was joined by Felia Litvin who sang the Russian National Anthem at the beginning of the programme; and the second on the 29th of the same month at the Paris Opera House. The latter was a matinée performance, for although the Opéra had just reopened, it did not resume its evening performances until six months later, and even then they were fated to be frequently interrupted by air raids by Gothas and Zeppelins.

These two festival performances marked Stravinsky's début as a conductor. At Geneva, he conducted a symphonic suite extracted from

The Fire Bird, while Ernest Ansermet, who had been appointed the chief conductor of the company, took over the rest of the programme. The Genevese public had to put up with a performance in costume but without scenery, since all the décor, most of it by celebrated Russian painters like Leon Bakst and Larionov, had remained in the store-rooms of the Palais Garnier since the last season of the Russian Ballet in 1914.

And so the Parisian public was able to enjoy in one programme two works of Rimsky-Korsakov, *Sheherazade* and *The Midnight Sun*, together with *The Sleeping Beauty* of Tchaikovsky, Borodin's Polovtsian Dances from *Prince Igor* and *The Fire Bird* conducted by the composer. A symphonic interlude from Rimsky-Korsakov's *Antar* and some Russian songs sung by Felia Litvin completed the programme, and the performance netted the fabulous sum of 400,000 gold francs (or £16,000) for the British Red Cross. In the middle of the War, Diaghilev's Russian Ballet had succeeded in recapturing all the lavish glamour of its pre-war seasons.

Three days later (1st January, 1916) the whole company sailed from Europe at a moment when the Atlantic was infested by enemy submarines.

Stravinsky, for his part, made good use of his trip to Paris by meeting a number of his friends. One of these was the Princess Edmond de Polignac, whose brilliant receptions, which before the war had been frequented by all the cream of Parisian society and the world of art, were momentarily in suspense. Despite this, the princess was anxious to promote a number of artistic projects, including various chamber opera performances that she intended to mount for the delectation of her guests once the war was over. At the Château d'Oex, Stravinsky had already started to sketch out a theatrical piece based on the theme of an old Russian story. This plan met with the princess's approval; and the composer returned from Paris to Morges anxious to forge ahead with his new task. *Reynard* (as the piece was called) proved to be another of Stravinsky's attempts to solve the problem of the alliance of music and drama—this time on quite different lines from *The Nightingale*.

Drawing by Picasso

DIVERSIONS

It has already been noticed how Stravinsky, like many great artists, is accustomed to relax between important works needing a long period of concentration by throwing off light works of lesser importance. This is the result of a natural reflex rather than wilful caprice. The creation of any important work, whether pictorial, literary or musical, is obsessive insofar as all artistic invention depends on the operation of choice. On the other hand, the relaxation brought about by the composition of a minor work may help to bring to light ideas that the artist has forgotten, and impressions or intentions he has hitherto neglected or repulsed. So, during the period that Stravinsky was engaged on two works of major importance, *viz. Reynard* and *The Wedding*, he produced a number of minor works which are of considerable significance in the light of his subsequent development.

First of all, a second collection of pieces for piano (four hands) entitled Five Easy Pieces, which could be looked on as a continuation of the vein of those Three Easy Pieces that had tickled Diaghilev's fancy, with this difference—that instead of being a group of portraits, the new group represented a witty stylisation of contemporary songs and dances. It would be no exaggeration to say that it was in a similar mood that the great Italian and French lutenists of the fifteenth and sixteenth centuries and clavichord composers of the eighteenth century like Frescobaldi and Couperin created the suite. From the time of Vincenzo Galilei (the father of the great scientist) to J. S. Bach, the Allemands, Bourrees, Galliards, Gigues that made up the various movements of the suite were merely popular dance forms that had been promoted by composers of talent to take their place among more learned art forms, thereby enriching the repertory of instrumental music. This tradition was renewed by the five pieces of this second collection, *viz.* Andante, Espagnola, Balalaika, Napolitana and Gallop, which are considerably more interesting than the pieces of the first collection and give the impression of being brief parerga thrown off as a temporary escape from Stravinsky's overwhelming occupation with folklore. In some ways they recall the atmosphere of an earlier Paris, of the pre-war city where the young musician from St. Petersburg enjoyed his first great public success.

The *Cat's Cradle Songs* bring one back to Russia once again with their warm, intimate domestic setting during a winter's evening. Beneath the singer's deep alto voice the purring of the cat who is asleep *On the Stove* can be distinguished in the tremolo of the three clarinets. Suddenly wakened by an unusual noise, puss goes off to crack nuts in a corner, while the kittens who want their share of the spoils peer anxiously after her. This *Interior Scene* is followed by a *Lullaby* in which a child is sung asleep, while the cat sets off, clad in her grey dress, to catch mice.

This suite was followed by *Three Tales for Children* which deal entertainingly with some of the animals that are so well beloved by children. The bustle of *Tilimbom* and the farmyard gabble of *Drakes, Geese and Swans* can be heard in the accompaniment that sounds just like a mechanical piano; and this reminds one that there was a time when Stravinsky had thought of using the pianola (then a new instrument) in his orchestration of *The Wedding*. (In any case he wrote a special Study for it later on in order to test its capacity.) The third of the songs is a frightening little story. It tells how a *Bear*—whose heavy footsteps are brought out by a rigorous bass *ostinato*—breaks into an isolated hut in the middle of a forest, where a poor old woodcutter and his wife are about to make their supper off the Bear's paw which the woodcutter had chopped off earlier in the day. The old man tries to hide under the kneading-trough; the old woman gets under the dirty linen: but in the end the Bear finds them both and gobbles them up.

Four Russian Peasant Songs for unaccompanied women's voices complete this group of miniature works: songs of hunting, fishing and sowing, and songs of divination used to accompany fortune telling, the whole larded with peasant humour and garnished with simple straight-forward music distinguished by delightfully original polyphonic touches.

TOLEDO AND THE ESCORIAL

At the end of the winter of 1916, Stravinsky was anxious for news of Diaghilev, who was then on the point of sailing from America with his company of ballet dancers. One day in March he received a message from Spain announcing Diaghilev's safe arrival and immediately left Switzerland for Madrid.

Diaghilev received him with open arms. A few days later, when the Russian Ballet was performing *The Fire Bird* and *Petrushka* at the Teatro Real, Stravinsky was presented to Alphonso XIII and the two Queens.

Although he displayed little interest in Spanish popular music, he was profoundly impressed by the Toledo of Ximenes (the Grand Inquisitor of the reign of Ferdinand the Catholic) and the Escorial of Philip II. Being himself a man of strong religious feelings, he was naturally struck by these eloquent examples of the Spanish feeling for mysticism, and their passionate exaltation reminded him of the fervent mysticism of his own native country.

On his return to Morges he rejoined Ramuz, and the two collaborators set to work to draw up the French text of *Reynard*, the composition of which was proceeding apace.

A MUSICAL FARCE

The plot of this burlesque is based on an episode in the story of Reynard the Fox, the origins of which can be traced back to Aesop's Fables. Although these fables became familiar to the writers of the Middle Ages in their classical guise, the fact that they are found, with variations, in the popular lore of every European nation, including the Finns and White Russians as well as the Italians, proves their common origin; and the idea of animals acting as protagonists in various adventures is also to be found in Asia. In any case, it was the crude and primitive aspect of the story that appealed to Stravinsky and which left its special imprint on his work.

The libretto, as drafted by Stravinsky himself, is simple in its outlines. By allusion rather than direct narrative, it tells the story of the misadventures of the Cock, a proud, vain character who is so extraordinarily stupid that on two occasions he allows himself to be taken in by the machinations of Reynard his enemy. Without the good offices of Frer Cat and Frer Goat, whose aid he implores, all would have been over! The essence of the piece lies in its moral. By his misdeeds Reynard has incurred the hatred of the animal world and is dragged out of his house, scratched, bitten and finally stoned by a gang of wild beasts. The commentator then makes a direct appeal to the audience's pockets, adding by way of final tag:—

> *If you've enjoyed this tale of the Fox,*
> *Drop your pennies in my box!*

To accompany this story, Stravinsky imagined a special kind of *mise en scène*. The spectacle was to be played by clowns, dancers and acrobats, while the text was entrusted to a quartet of men's voices placed in the orchestra. This arrangment led to the dissociation of the musical element from the visual and was at complete variance with the realistic tradition in the theatre. It had a number of advantages, of which the more obvious was that it allowed the players on the stage to indulge in the sort of mime that was appropriate to the fantasy world of animals —an impossibility for singers themselves—and this could be related to circus technique rather than dance choreography. Moreover, such a method of presentation allowed the music to preserve its formal autonomy in the same way as a painter like Picasso might be said to aim at safeguarding the formal independence of his painting from representational compromise. Henceforward, this preoccupation with the need to subordinate the spectacle to the music will be found increasingly to dominate Stravinsky's attitude to the theatre.

Like *The Wedding*, the score of *Reynard* is full of songs. Nevertheless they are treated in a very different way from the polyphonc and instrumental standpoints. In view of the archaic origin of the story, the composer allowed himself to be inspired by certain primitive technical procedures without trying literally to reproduce them in his score. His main preoccupation was to avoid the use of chords, which were unknown to the singers of the Middle Ages. So he used a polyphony made up by combining different musical voices, some of them polytonal, others polymodal, and this resulted in a curious amalgam which might easily sound empty or crude to ears accustomed to (and, possibly, abused by) the harmonic tradition of the immediate past. As far as comparison can legitimately be made between music and the fine arts, it may be said that the effect of this music is similar to the feeling of confusion sometimes experienced when one is confronted by a work of Byzantine art in which the notion of perspective is completely lacking.

The vigorous touch and corrosive tang resulting from this special type of polyphony were accentuated by certain instrumental features such as the raucous pitch of the Eb clarinet, the metallic sonority of the cimbalom etc. Stravinsky had first heard the latter instrument in a Genevese restaurant and was so enchanted by it that he could not rest until he had obtained one for his own use. Mention should also be made of the drum roll that, in accordance with circus tradition, accompanies the two passages in the score (marked *salto mortale*) where the Cock foolishly jumps from his perch, only to be caught immediately by Reynard his enemy.

And so, for various reasons, some of them connected with the stage spectacle, others with the music, *Reynard* is quite different from Stravinsky's preceding works. The note of buffoonery that had already made its appearance in earlier works was here transformed into a sort of musical farce reminiscent of medieval satires. *Reynard* is an extremely successful piece with a new caustic turn of wit and freshness of sound, and its music undoubtedly profited by the severe restrictions laid upon it. There is no touch of caricature, no hint of plagiarism, in the score, which expresses to perfection one of the most attractive sides of Stravinsky's musical personality.

DREAMS

The news of the Russian Revolution of March 1917 threw Stravinsky into considerable agitation. In his youth about the only place where he had found encouragement for his ambition to be a composer was the house of his uncle Ielachich,—and it might have been thought that this fact should have disposed him in favour of the intellectual classes in St. Petersburg made up of magistrates, civil servants and lawyers, whose influence at that time seemed to be growing steadily,—nevertheless from the beginning he had nourished an instinctive dislike for the advanced ideas fermenting around him, and this feeling was only confirmed by mature reflection in later life. The critical opposition of the so-called intelligentsia to imperial authority, the spread of progressive doctrines as a result of allegiance to the equalitarian principles of the 'rights of man', and above all the abominable plague of atheism which was so prevalent in middle-class circles at that time, aroused his increasing antipathy.

But now all that was going to be changed! On a March day in 1917, walking up a hill near Morges with their voices raised above the bitter *bise*, Ramuz and Stravinsky discussed these matters with impassioned interest, dreaming of the birth of a new Russia which would no longer be polluted by the European slime that had been deposited in the country during the previous two centuries. A bureaucratic system imported from Germany, a certain liberalism in politics borrowed from the Anglo-Saxon world, and a ridiculous belief in progress derived from materialist science—all these were calamities that had unfortunately combined to stifle the native virtues of the Russian people. Yes, Russia was to return to the untarnished sources of its true past—long before the time of Peter the Great—a past to which *The Wedding* rightly belonged. And then Russia would be able to face a fresh future—a new State where all the great Russians of the past—Pushkin, Gogol, Mussorgsky—would take their rightful place: a Russia which above all would return to Christianity.

So it was with a mind full of hope and even of plans for returning to Russia and to his family estate at Ustilug that Stravinsky set off on his second visit to Rome where he had been summoned by Diaghilev.

FROM ROME TO NAPLES WITH COCTEAU AND PICASSO

It had been arranged that the Russian Ballet should open its season at the Teatro Costanzi with a gala performance in aid of the Red Cross. On such an occasion it is customary to play the appropriate national anthems. But what could be done in view of recent events? *God save the Tsar* was clearly impossible because of Nicholas II's recent abdication. Diaghilev suddenly had the idea to replace the invalid Russian national anthem by a well-known popular tune, *The Song of the Volga Boatmen*. But time was short and it would have to be specially orchestrated. So it came about that the night before the performance, Stravinsky, sitting at the piano, dictated to Ansermet, chord by chord, the instrumentation of this popular song, which partnered the Italian national anthem the following evening before the curtain went up.

Despite wartime exigencies, Diaghilev always behaved like a perfect host and treated his guests and collaborators with exquisite hospitality. It was on one of these occasions that Stravinsky first met Pablo Picasso, Bolla the futurist, Jean Cocteau and Lord Berners, who were among Diaghilev's guests. From Rome the company moved on to Naples where Picasso and Stravinsky, visiting the aquarium together and haunting the antique shops, laid the foundations of an enduring friendship.

While it is very tempting at first to trace a parallel between Picasso and Stravinsky, on closer examination it becomes extremely difficult, despite surface resemblances, to illustrate this apposition, especially in terms of the different techniques applicable to the two arts concerned, for the visible world of the fine arts is separated from the audible world of music by an abyss. It might be argued, for instance, that in the same way as Stravinsky overthrew harmonic unity by his use of polytonality, Picasso broke up objective unity by his use of cubism as in paintings like *La Reine Isabeau* (1909) and *Nature morte à la guitare* (1913). Nevertheless, these are two very different tendencies, for in the case of Picasso the dislocation occurs in connection with the natural vision of ordinary objects and defies the laws of common sense, while the composer is merely attacking habits of listening which, however well established, can be easily transformed, since they are allied to no natural phenomenon. The ear is much more adaptable than the eye.

But there is another point, where (according to Stravinsky) the two artists meet. For both of them the work of creation is seen as a problem to be solved. The nature of this problem is explicit and concerns the tendency of the work created to free itself from the domination of its subject matter. This principle had already been enunciated by Cézanne before Picasso, and traces of it can be found in Mallarmé's poetic theory and practice which led towards an abstract music made up of words, phonics and rhythms rather than the clear and logical expression of concrete ideas. Insofar as Mallarmé's critics and interpreters found, or believed they had found this technique intelligible, the music of the verse functioned like a screen interposed between the projection of the poet's inspiration and the poem's ultimate form.

73

It might be objected that such abstract poetic or pictorial trans-figurations could have no relationship with music, since music is incapable of representing anything at all. But it must not be forgotten that this autonomy, so recently acquired by poetry and the visual arts, has for long been accepted as an attribute of music since it dates from the conscious process of stylisation adopted by some of the earliest composers of suites. Without entering into a disquisition about the fundamental links between music and mime, one may notice elsewhere signs of this autonomy in Stravinsky's music—in the liberties he takes with prosody, and in the unrealistic spectacle and action of works like *Reynard*, *The Wedding* and *The Soldier's Tale*, which are all examples of the independence of the music from its theme.

In any case, however different a musical subject may be from a poetic or pictorial subject, the subject exists in its own right so that even if the problems to be solved are not identical in the cases of Picasso and Stravinsky, at least they are parallel. And when it is remembered that Picasso's work had been familiar to Stravinsky since the beginning of the century, there is nothing astonishing in the fact that traces of Picasso's influence can be found in Stravinsky's music before the meeting of the two artists in Naples.

There is nothing absurd in talking about cubism in connection with *Reynard* or *The Wedding*, for these works show the same preoccupation with formal problems as the *Nature mort à la tête de mort* (1907) or the *Femme à la mandoline* (1909). As for the joker who called *Les Demoiselles d'Avignon* 'a pictorial Rite of Spring', he was nearer the truth than might at first appear. Picasso's composition owed much to negro and Poly-nesian masks (or, possibly, to the masklike faces of archaic Egyptian or Greek art): but little notice has been paid to the strange resemblance between some passages of *The Rite of Spring*—particularly the intro-duction—and certain kinds of primitive music. This resemblance has only recently come to light, thanks to the discoveries made by musical ethnology. Its importance is all the greater because much of Stravinsky's output during his period of residence in the Vaud was written in a deliberately primitive idiom.

Quite soon Picasso and Stravinsky were to become collaborators in a joint theatrical enterprise: but meanwhile it is time to drop this digres-sion on aesthetics and return to Naples.

There Stravinsky attended the rehearsals of *The Good Humoured Ladies*, a ballet that Massine was mounting on music of Scarlatti orches-trated by Tomasini. (A few years later Stravinsky was to recall the pleasure he had derived from this production at a moment when Diaghilev broached the subject of *Pulcinella*, a work which was destined to be of special significance in his musical output because it marked an important change of artistic direction.)

Drawing by Picasso, 1917

On his return to Switzerland, he was interrogated by the Customs officials at Chiasso, and the following dialogue took place.

'What is this sketch?'

'My portrait drawn by Picasso.'

'Nonsense. It must be a plan.'

'Yes—the plan of my face.'

The frontier authorities were not convinced. In their view, this portrait with its firm and rather geometrical outline could depict nothing except a plan of some secret work of military importance. And Stravinsky had to have recourse to the good offices of his friend Lord Berners to arrange for the drawing's despatch by the British Embassy in Rome before he was able to recover this precious token of his new friendship.

Cover for 'Ragtime' designed by Picasso

TRIBULATIONS OF A TOURING THEATRE

The second half of 1917 was marked by a number of disasters: first of all the death of an old servant of the Stravinsky household who had entered his parents' service before he was born; then the death of his brother Gury who succumbed to typhus on the Rumanian front; and finally the October Revolution in Russia which led not only to the

Ramuz, Auberjonois, Stravinsky, Ansermet, Ludmilla Pitöeff (painting on glass by Auberjonois, 1918)

dispersal of his dreams and hopes, but also to the collapse of his personal finances. He was cut off from all his possessions in Russia and found himself without means of subsistence in a foreign country in the middle of a seemingly endless war.

He was not the only one to suffer in this way. Ramuz, Ansermet and many of his other friends were in a similar plight. The musical life of that part of Switzerland had almost completely ceased; orchestras were disbanded, the theatres had closed down. There was no artistic interchange with neighbouring countries. It was in the course of numerous talks held by Stravinsky's little group of friends that the idea of creating a touring theatre to meet the needs of a public that had been almost completely deprived of entertainment was discussed. The generous

support of Werner Reinhart of Winterthur, a man of broad culture, the personal friend of many artists, and a clarinettist of considerable ability, was enlisted for this project; and these unusual circumstances brought about the creation of a strange work, *The Soldier's Tale*, a story to be read, played and danced.

When elaborating this new project, which (like some of Stravinsky's other recent works) was based on a folk story, Ramuz and Stravinsky decided to be strictly practical. It was naturally important to attract the public, even in the smallest villages, and so by common consent priority was given to the element of narrative as entrusted to the reader, with the music intervening like a series of illustrations only when the narrative became heightened into drama and produced a little scene susceptible of stylised treatment.

The collaborators did not attempt to remove the various naiveties from this fireside story, which tells of a curious sort of soldier who marches for days on end towards his native village (music: 'The Soldier's March'), takes a violin out of his pack to amuse himself while he rests by the banks of a stream (music: a kind of concertino with much double-stopping for the violin). This violin seems to be a rather special kind of instrument, perhaps a symbol, for the Devil uses all his wiles to get possession of it. Having bartered it ('Pastoral') the Soldier renews his march (repeat of the opening March). Thanks to a talisman which he has obtained in exchange for his violin, he becomes rich—very rich— too rich, for as is usually the case in these moral folk stories, he becomes tired of all his wealth and ends by rejecting it and so breaking the spell. Suddenly, as if by magic, he finds himself in a Royal Palace ('The Royal March') where he renews his acquaintance with the Devil, wins back his violin (another concertino), charms a young and ailing princess and makes love to her ('Tango—Waltz—Ragtime'). He marries her, and dissatisfied by his newly acquired happiness, decides to return to his past and revisit his native village. But as Ramuz's text says '*A single happiness is happiness complete: a second happiness cancels out the first.*' And the Devil takes advantage of the fact that by imprudently crossing the boundary of his new dominions the unfortunate Soldier has put himself in his power ('Triumphal March of the Devil').

From this summary, it will be seen that the score consists of a succession of different numbers, each with its appropriate character and form. It is founded on the principle of the suite, which had already been used as the basic form of the two collections of Easy Pieces for piano duet; and in retrospect these two suites appear like preliminary experiments that were to lead to *The Soldier's Tale*.

Although the polyphonic style of the new work was closely related to that of *Reynard*—which was natural in view of the popular source of each subject—the two scores were really very different. With *The Soldier's Tale* the basic material was no longer Russian folk song; but a simple march tune tricked out with military fanfares was followed by

Morges, 1916

another march tune based on a Spanish pasodoble, and in the dance numbers a Viennese waltz was flanked by an Argentinian tango and an American rag-time. Despite the disparity of this heterogeneous material, Stravinsky succeeded in achieving complete unity of style—and this miracle was intensified by his use of a most unusual orchestra with trombone, double-bass and violin on the conductor's left, bassoon in front, and percussion, cornet and clarinet on his right. It might have been thought that with such an orchestra it would have been difficult to obtain a proper balance—nevertheless, he found a perfect solution to this problem in his instrumentation of the two chorales that accompany the love scene of the Soldier and the Princess.

The first performance of *The Soldier's Tale*, which took place at the Lausanne Theatre on 28th September, 1918, was one of the few occasions on which Stravinsky declared himself fully satisfied with the stage presentation of one of his works. Neither Fokine's choreography for *The Fire Bird* nor Nijinsky's for *The Rite of Spring* nor Fokine's crowd movements in *Petrushka* had found favour with him. But in the case of *The Soldier's Tale*, he was full of praise for Ansermet the conductor, Georges and Ludmilla Pitoëff and the rest of the cast, and also for René Auberjonois, who had designed the scenery and costumes.

Flushed with success, the company's future looked rosy. Posters announcing its arrival covered the walls of a number of towns, and various halls had been booked in advance. A van was to have been used to transport the company with its scenery and props. But in the event all these plans had to be abandoned.

The frightful slaughter of the War had brought in its train another plague—Spanish influenza—an epidemic of which broke out in Europe that autumn. Although Switzerland had succeeded in keeping out of the War, it was unable to keep this scourge at bay. Gradually all public activity was paralysed. The van never took to the road. One after another the members of the company caught influenza. Even Stravinsky himself succumbed.

Immediately after finishing the score of *The Soldier's Tale*, he composed a *Ragtime* for eleven instruments (wind, strings, cymbalom and percussion), the last notes of which were written down at 11 a.m. on 11th November, 1918, at the very moment the armistice was being signed.

Farewells

Detail from the drop-curtain by Matisse for 'The Song of the Nightingale', 1920

Farewells

The convulsion had been too deep, the misery too widespread for an immediate return to normal life to be possible, even in a neutral country like Switzerland. Considerable confusion was created by a railway strike, the uproar caused by the repatriation of prisoners of war, and the civil disorders that broke out in Germany. Nevertheless the day came at last when the barriers between Vaud and the rest of the world were down; and then Stravinsky, who had been incapacitated by illness for several weeks, was at last able to return to his desk.

This was a remarkable work-table, with its bottles of black, green, red and blue ink in serried ranks, its collection of erasors of various kinds, pen-holders, drawing pens (one for quavers, another for semi-quavers), not to forget the 'stravigor' for ruling staves, an invention of Stravinsky's own. All these objects had a precise purpose, helping to express the composer's inspiration through the movements of his hands and symbolising order, method, and thought directed to a clearly established end. The focus of all this spiritual activity was in the page of manuscript orchestral score lying on the composer's desk, and this was invariably a masterpiece of musical calligraphy.

But the shock had been a heavy one; and for the time being the composer felt too weak to undertake anything of major importance. The orchestration of the first two of the Three Pieces for String Quartet written in 1914, the composition of the Four Russian Songs, the Three Pieces for Clarinet Solo, and the reorchestration of *The Fire Bird* suite for medium orchestra filled the comparatively quiet months between the end of 1918 and the following May.

Only five years had passed since *The Rite of Spring*—but what a lifetime they spanned! None who experienced those years of war, whether at close quarters or from a distance, could remain unaffected by them; and this was certainly the case with Stravinsky. Traces of anguish and sorrow arising from his memory of former days were to be found in his work. Listen to the words of the Dissenting Song, the last of his Four Russian Songs, which marked his return to creative activity:—

> Wind, snow, darkness;
> All roads, all my paths, are closed.
> It is impossible to travel
> On foot or by carriage
> The ways that lead
> To the life-giving Heavenly King—
> Impassable to me, my fellow brethren,
> Brothers in love, brothers in spirit,
> Chosen by Holy God Himself.
> But Glory be to the Father
> And power to Jesus Christ,
> Glory to God—Glory to God.
> World without end.
> Amen.
> We honour Thee O Lord.★

It is difficult not to hear, through the words of this Dissenting Song, the creator of *The Wedding*, *Pribaoutki*, the *Cat's Cradle Songs* and *Reynard* bidding a moving, almost mystic, farewell to Russia his native land.

Henceforward, no echo of Russia was to be found in his music, with the exception of *The Fairy's Kiss* which ten years later would be written and dedicated to the memory of Tchaikovsky and reveal a gentle nostalgia for the past.from which Stravinsky had then become totally estranged.

JAZZ

The word 'ragtime' is now so familiar that readers may have paid little or no attention to it when it was mentioned above in connection with *The Soldier's Tale*; but when Stravinsky first made use of it, it was
★Translated from the Russian by Sarah S. White.

a completely unknown type of music in Europe. He probably first encountered it in some sheet music that Ernest Ansermet brought back with him from America towards the end of the War and was immediately captivated by the novelty of its syncopated rhythms. Nevertheless he did not set about making use of it straightaway. At that moment he was preoccupied by various important works, probably *Reynard* and *The Wedding*, and he was not likely to be distracted by this novelty while still under the spell of Russia and her folklore. But by the time he started work on *The Soldier's Tale*, the situation had completely changed, for by then the psychological crisis mentioned above had taken place; and his first piece of ragtime showed that he had closely studied the jazz publications received from America. But this preliminary essay did not satisfy his appetite. During the preparations at Lausanne for the production of *The Soldier's Tale*, he drafted the *Ragtime* for eleven instruments, just before succumbing to influenza. Six months later, the *Piano-Rag-Music* (dedicated to Arthur Rubinstein) showed his increasing interest in the rhythmic structure of jazz with its use of syncopation which he enjoyed employing on different levels, enriching the modulations with polytonal passages, and allowing his imagination to be stimulated in various other ways by this new idiom

Just as after *Petrushka* he used Russian folklore, both literary and musical, as basic material for his compositions, so now he turned to jazz. The creative process appeared as an effort of stylisation, a method of synthesising these raw materials; and this was developed to a point where all undesirable elements could be eliminated—such as, for instance, the harmonic banalities of earliest jazz with their mechanical cadences, which he completely transformed.

There is no need to argue that the introduction of this element of roughage into Stravinsky's musical language was any more prejudicial to the quality of his art than the use by painters like Toulouse-Lautrec or Picasso of low-life subjects drawn from fairgrounds or dance halls. The strength of art lies in its ability to transform the basic materials it uses; and in this process the materials shed the implications of their 'subject matter' in the conventional sense of that expression. It is enough to say that jazz seemed to open up new perspectives in Stravinsky's field of composition and helped him to free himself from the folklore material he had relied on during the last four years. And this change of direction from the east to the west was about to be clinched by a business proposal from Diaghilev.

It was at the beginning of the first post-war spring of 1919, in the course of a brief trip to Paris, that the two friends met again. They had not seen each other for over a year and the first thing Stravinsky did was to tell Diaghilev about the success of *The Soldier's Tale* at Lausanne; but Diaghilev's character was such that he was unable to admit that members of his team should work for others than himself, so Stravinsky's story had a cool reception. On the other hand he had a proposal

Matisse and Massine, Monte-Carlo, 1920

to make—he suggested that Stravinsky's opera *The Nightingale* should be turned into a ballet with décor by Henri Matisse and choreography by Massine. Despite its surface attractions, this project did not really tempt Stravinsky who considered the static nature of the music unsuited to the dance requirements of a ballet.

At this point, Diaghilev recalled the success of *The Good Humoured Ladies* based on a score adapted from pieces by Scarlatti, which had been given in Rome two years earlier. Since then he had collected copies of a number of Pergolesi manuscripts from various libraries in Italy and London; and he showed these to his friend, suggesting they should be used as the basis of a score for a ballet in the Italian style. This was the genesis of *Pulcinella* and the beginning of Stravinsky's flirtation with Italian music which was to lead to the awakening of a number of kindred characteristics in his own idiom.

Back at Morges, he hastened to complete his *Piano-Rag-Music* so as to be able to start at once on the music to accompany this *commedia dell'arte* ballet. The prospect of working with Picasso and renewing contact with Paris which was rapidly becoming the artistic centre of the world gave him a special stimulus. Although he spent the greater part of the following twelve months at Morges, in spirit he was already in Paris; and it was soon decided that the whole family should move to France, which was to become his adopted country for the next twenty years.

Stravinsky, Diaghilev, Cocteau and Satie (Larionov)

Jean Cocteau

'Impressionism has just let off its rockets at the end of a long fête. It's for us to prepare the fireworks for another fête.' So wrote Jean Cocteau in March 1918 in a booklet called *Le Coq et l'Arlequin* which created a considerable stir at the time. In these 'marginal notes to music', the gifted author poured forth a succession of aphorisms which were to become the bible of the young French musicians of that period.

The first cardinal principle was to avoid being a Wagnerite. 'To defend Wagner because he's attacked by Saint-Saëns is too simple. We must cry with Saint-Saëns "Down with Wagner!" That's the courageous line to take!' Brangäne's magic philtre was out—so were all the spells of old Klingsor, including the charm of the Flower Maidens. To try to penetrate the fogs surrounding *The Ring* was unfashionable. One must avoid this suspect 'music of the bowels' whose effect was like that of a conjuring trick, this 'music to be listened to with head in hands'. All this was in line with Debussy's views—in fact the whole body of Debussy's work could be looked on as a reaction against Wagner's

◀ *Stravinsky and Cocteau at the Festival de l'oeuvre du XX siècle, 1948* conception of art. In *Le Coq et l'Arlequin* matters were not quite as simple as all that, for 'impressionism is the counterblast to Wagner, the last peals of thunder after the storm', and—unexpected though it may appear—*Pelléas* in its turn is 'music to be listened to with head in hands'. And not only *Pelléas*, but also *The Rite!* 'I look on *The Rite* as a masterpiece,' says Cocteau, 'but the atmosphere that has been built up round its performances reminds me of a religious conspiracy between initiates, like the hypnotic spell of Bayreuth.'

Debussy and Stravinsky relegated to the same category as Wagner—that was a serious matter indeed! For that meant that their works were no longer being judged objectively, but in the light of public reaction. What then was to be done? How was one not to incur the reproach of being a hypnotist, a bogus romantic or (what might be worse) one of the late adherents of impressionism and imprecision? If *Le Coq et l'Arlequin* rejected with equal disdain 'the fogs of Wagner' which blotted out the pathway and 'the mists of Debussy' which brought infection, if the listener had had 'enough of clouds, waves, aquariums, water-sprites and night-scents', what could be put in their place? Stravinsky's *Reynard*, *The Wedding*, or *The Soldier's Tale* or perhaps the *Pribaoutki*? Certainly not, for at that moment those works were still unknown. And even had they been known, they would not have met the case, for their music was far from providing the lost treasure of simplicity in all its essential purity and clarity, 'the only possible counterpoise to a period of extreme refinement'. So high did the Cocteau of *Le Coq et l'Arlequin* set the concept of simplicity that he included in his booklet a little glossary of words and expressions to show that 'simplicity should not be looked on as being synonymous with poverty, nor as a retrograde step'.

At that moment only one musician could boast of this precious quality of simplicity, and that was Erik Satie, the composer of *Morceaux en forme de poire*, which had been the butt of so much scorn, and who had just written his masterpiece, *Parade*, in collaboration with Cocteau—a work which was praised in *Le Coq et l'Arlequin* for sounding like 'a steam organ laden with dreams'. I'm not sure whether, in order to understand *Parade*, it is necessary (as Cocteau suggests) 'to start as far back as Adam and Eve'—which would take rather a long time; but remembering Cocteau's remark that 'every cry of *Long Live X!* implies a cry of *Down with Y!*' my first impression is that the main purpose of the Cocteau-Satie axis must have been to proclaim aloud and abroad *Down with Y!* But on reflection I think this imputes somewhat too much significance to *Parade*, which after all was only a minor work, a practical joke played by a couple of slightly malicious children at the expense of their elders—the critics, the snobs and the aesthetes. One thing at least is certain, Satie's was not the sort of score 'to be listened to with head in hands'. I will say no more for fear of saying too much, and I will merely mention the fact that the first performance of *Parade*, which was given on 18th May 1917 on the occasion of a visit of the Russian Ballet to Paris, was a miscalculation on Diaghilev's part, despite Picasso's brilliant contribution. This was not the right moment for lighthearted jokes, and the public failed to appreciate the flavour of pregnant simplicity that it was offered in the antics of the Little Girl 'riding a race, going for a bicycle ride, boxing, dancing a ragtime', and all the conjuring tricks of the Chinaman and other bits of like facetiousness.

But all that was of little significance. What really mattered was that under Cocteau's auspices was formed *Les Six* (in imitation of the Russian group of the Mighty Five) and these musicians were destined to play a part—some of them an important one—in the French contemporary musical scene. Nor did all of the six blindly follow the lead given by their spokesman towards the ideal of new simplicity.

It is true that in addition to its moments of exaggeration *Le Coq et l'Arlequin* contained a number of good points—it was distinguished by its youthful verve, a dry and ready wit, a readiness to juggle with meanings and to take advantage of misunderstandings, all of them qualities that were closely allied to the spirit of the Italian *Commedia dell'arte* and in particular the Neapolitan aspect of it, with which Cocteau, Picasso and Stravinsky had become acquainted at the time of their meeting in Italy in 1917.. And it is easy to understand how Cocteau who (as he has told us) 'admires the harlequins of Cézanne and Picasso, but not Harlequin himself' came to be the link between the two Stravinskys: the old Stravinsky, who was the only one known to the public at that moment, the interpreter of barbarous, primitive Russia, and the new Stravinsky who was about to confound his admirers with *Pulcinella*.

PETRUSHKA'S COUSIN

'It was as if the critics and the smart set had just managed to learn an extremely complicated game of bezique and were beginning to boast of their prowess, when they were baffled by the game being suddenly changed to leapfrog.' This quotation from a lecture given by Jean Cocteau at the Collège de France in 1923 could be applied to the reception given to *Pulcinella*. After their initial dislike and misunderstanding of the work, the critics and the public had ended by accepting *The Rite*: but now Stravinsky the *fauve*, who had revivified the musical language with his inventions of new harmonies and new rhythms, served up a *pastiche*. This is perhaps too severe a judgment and one that needs reconsideration now that a point has been reached, from which the work can be viewed in a different perspective, particularly since this judgment has been rigorously contested by many of Stravinsky's interpreters.

Disapproval was certainly not due merely to the fact that the score was founded on themes by Pergolesi. Many other works by Stravinsky had borrowed material from outside sources, from folk music in particular, and also from popular songs and dances, without the slightest danger of the resulting scores being dubbed *pastiche*, since in their case the basic materials had always been successfully transmuted by the polyphonic treatment they received. It was precisely this element of transmutation that was lacking in *Pulcinella*, since Stravinsky elected not merely to use tunes by Pergolesi as the basis for his new work, but also to reconstitute the style of the Italian composer and his period— that is to say to adopt the way Pergolesi's melodies unfolded, developed and were articulated, the one with the other, a procedure which was naturally bound up with a particular harmonic climate, completely alien to the Russian composer, and which inevitably led to something which Stravinsky and other contemporary composers had already rejected—namely, the language of conventional tonality. So unexpected an attitude was bound to appear in the eyes of the public an unaccountable *volte face*. No one outside the circle of Stravinsky's initiates was likely to realise that there had been a 'change of game', or that there was even any question of playing a game in this score that exploits a vein of malice and sarcasm, enjoyed at the expense of others, which is one of the dominating factors of Italian comedy, as for instance in Pergolesi's *La Serva Padrona*, a work that helped to precipitate the *Guerre des Bouffons* in Paris in the eighteenth century.

In view of the public's widespread ignorance at that moment of all the works Stravinsky had written in Switzerland, how could it possibly have been expected to recognise in the samewhat caustic wit of *Pulcinella*, in the sparkling resourcefulness of this fantasy, a metamorphosis of *Pribaoutki, Reynard* and the straight-face humour of the Easy Pieces for Piano, which had so completely mystified Diaghilev when he found himself cast for the role of a circus ring-master? How could it have guessed that, in handling these melodies by Pergolesi, Stravinsky had felt awaken in him through the intermediary of Petrushka, Pulcinella's Russian cousin, an affinity of mind with the Italian artistic tradition that had reigned supreme in the Russia of Peter the Great? That was why the 'game of leap-frog' that was suddenly suggested to the public—or, let us rather call it the reincarnation of a musical idiom that had become academic in the course of time—was bound at first to prove a disappointment.

Nevertheless, *Pulcinella* was something more than a *pastiche*. Looked at in the general context of Stravinsky's work, it was the forerunner of a new Italianate style brought in to fertilise the composer's musical thought—one of the two main currents to be observed in his music, which was often to influence it for the better but sometimes for the worse. For, in addition to lightness and vivacity, Italian art possesses the quality of facility, twin sister to the simplicity so much extolled by Cocteau, and this sometimes results in weakness and flabbiness, or even baroque exuberance, and sometimes degenerates into the superficiality of coloratura and mere vocal exercises.

Forty years later, the idea prevalent in 1920 that *Pulcinella* was a *pastiche* seems to have lost its importance, at least insofar as the score itself is concerned; and this musical evocation of the Italian eighteenth century, transfigured by Stravinsky's rhythmic invention, which is as witty as his instrumentation is piquant, can be viewed today with the same dispassionate pleasure as the neo-classical paintings of Picasso.

Costumes by Picasso for 'Pulcinella'

REGRETS

The time had not yet come for Stravinsky to pursue the new direction opened up by *Pulcinella*. Nevertheless, he was clearly delighted to have this Italian exercise as an excuse to renew his contact with the life of the theatre.

His next two works, however—the Concertino for String Quartet and the Symphonies of Wind Instruments—though differing from each other in many ways, shared a feeling of austerity and also a primitive harshness of timbre, which might have been due to his regret at leaving Vaud when he moved to France in the summer of 1920, settling first at Carantec and subsequently at Garches, or to his grief for the death of Debussy. This led him like a number of other eminent composers to agree to contribute to a special number of the *Revue Musicale*, a short piece dedicated to Debussy's memory. Probably both nostalgia and grief played their part in his musical thought.

Design by Picasso (1925)

As for the Concertino, it is of little relative importance to know that it is constructed on the plan of a sonata allegro with the central development replaced by a concertante passage for the first violin. The essential quality of the work is to be found elsewhere—in the special treatment of the strings. These have lost the qualities that used to be looked on as their special glory: their sweetness, their enveloping charm (so much beloved by the Impressionist School and to be found even in *The Rite of Spring* in a movement such as '*Cercles Mystérieux des Adolescentes*'), their languor which characterised so many dream-like Adagios, and naturally also their fire and attack which were sometimes used to excess by the romantic composers. In the Concertino, the strings are closely related to the soldier's violin in *The Soldier's Tale* and display the characteristic qualities of a village fiddler who is more concerned with roughly marking out the rhythm than with any refinement of playing or interpretation. Insofar as the musical idiom of the Concertino is essentially a rustic one it is related in certain ways to that of *The Wedding* and *Reynard*, but stripped of any folklore quality.

The germ of the Symphonies of Wind Instruments was the chorale that appeared in the Revue Musicale of 1st December, 1920—a succession of austere chords that Stravinsky used to frame the complete work, like an alley of funereal cypress trees. Bursts of fanfares, cries (like that of Nastasia Timofeevna at the beginning of *The Wedding*) alternated with liturgical passages for flutes and clarinets like pastoral garlands, and these different ingredients combined to produce a kind of violent combat where blocks of different sonorities clashed against each other in a breathless rhythm closely allied to that of the final movement of *The Rite of Spring*. Although it is naturally impossible to label each of the themes and there is certainly no question of direct imitation, the result is like an evocation of the thoughts of the earlier Stravinsky, revealing his love of nature and perhaps even something of his struggle against death.

The Concertino is a much more abstract piece and is related to the enigmatic cantata *The King of the Stars* through the Three Pieces for String Quartet of 1914. But if the Concertino and the Symphonies are looked upon from another angle, both seem to be suffused by the same mood of farewell, for at the end of 1921, when he wrote the final chord of the Symphonies, he had reached a point where he was cutting himself off, for many years to come, from the primitive subject matter that he had exploited with such consummate success in the past.

THE MOMENT OF CHOICE

During the winter season of 1920-21, Diaghilev undertook to mount a new production of *The Rite of Spring* at the Théâtre des Champs-Elysées with choreography by Massine, Nijinsky's version having lapsed owing to the mental illness that had overtaken him during the last few years. But at this time the Russian Ballet was considerably restricted in its touring plans. Germany and the other Central European countries had temporarily to be written off owing to the severe economic and social disorders resulting from their defeat. And Russia was completely isolated. As a result, Paris, benefitting from its privileged position, became the artistic centre of the world, and its social life was marked by a brilliant succession of receptions, soirées and every kind of festivity planned round a number of persons of exceptional talent, among whom Stravinsky was one of the most outstanding. Surrounded by admiration and adulation, at the summit of his fame, in full possession of his technical resources, the young maestro of thirty-eight was at this moment in some ways comparable to an Asiatic nabob who had suddenly wearied of his great wealth. Having adopted France as his second fatherland, he was obliged by circumstances to accept the view that Western Europe was cut off from his native land; and the result—of little significance perhaps from the point of view of world affairs, but of considerable importance from the aesthetic standpoint—was that everything in his art that hitherto had shown a national tinge now seemed to him to be an exotic excrescence. Fascinated by the gift of perpetual renewal so gracefully displayed by Cocteau and Picasso, and captivated by the recollection of his own success with *Pulcinella*, he decided to make a tremendous effort of renunciation. He would detach himself from his old loyalties; and henceforward all his speculative powers would be concentrated on the effort to evolve a new style which he intended should be classical and of universal appeal.

AN IMAGINARY MUSICAL MUSEUM

The result was as if he had decided to make a leisurely progress through the galleries of an imaginary musical museum in order to scrutinise the great figures of the past in an attempt to discover the secret of their genius. Bach, Pergolesi, Handel, Weber, Beethoven, Rossini, Donizetti and Verdi, and many others were evoked and their works laid under contribution. In other words, Stravinsky attempted to base his new creations on existing 'musical models'. Forms that had already been worked out in terms of sound were substituted for subjects derived from a universe outside the realm of music through direct observation, actual experience or mere imagination, as provided by visions, scenarios, poetic texts or even simple psychological states of mind; and this meant that his creative activity functioned at second hand.

This procedure is certainly analagous to that of many painters— Delacroix, for instance, Courbet, Renoir, Manet especially, for his *Déjeuner sur l'Herbe* was made up of recollections of Giorgione and Raphael, the serving maid in his *Bon Bock* was like a figure in a painting by Franz Hals, and his *Olympia* was based on copies he had made ten years previously of the Venus of Urbino and the Danae of Titian in the Naples Museum. Picasso himself in his perpetual quest for novelty was quite prepared to use the pictures of the old masters as a pretext for his own speculations, and in the process they were usually radically transformed. There would accordingly seem to be nothing particularly reprehensible in this principle of basing one's compositions on existing musical models (and by adopting it, it should be noted, Stravinsky helped to emphasise the basic affinity that has already been mentioned as existing between his art and that of Picasso). If one needed reassurance, one might point to the convincing example of Mozart who while trying all his life to write like other composers only succeeded in writing in the style of Mozart. But in Mozart's case it should be remembered that his inspiration came from his contemporaries and not from masters long since dead. Furthermore, as it had never been his intention to overthrow the idiom of his day, it is clear that by accepting and assimilating certain technical processes, he was in no way going counter to his own genius, but he was, if anything, enlarging his musical capacity.

It was quite different with Stravinsky; for here was an example not only of someone turning to the past—in this case, a relatively distant past—but also of a complete change of climate and the abandonment of one form of musical culture for another. This is indubitably a most difficult operation, a kind of mental metamorphosis. Imagine a Red Indian, a Pygmy, or a Bushman sitting at the feet of one of our Western European masters of music! A far-fetched idea perhaps, but one which throws psychological light on the problem involved. A twentieth-century man of intelligence, whether a musician or merely a listener, cannot forget that the astonishing composer of *The Rite of Spring* who created a whole new range of music including *Reynard*, *The Wedding* and *The Soldier's Tale*, owed the strength and freshness of his art to a spiritual inheritance reaching back to an era of Slav culture before the period of Peter the Great and the Europeanisation of Russia about which he complained so bitterly during the period of his exile in the Canton of Vaud. Whatever the reason was—whether vexation at the ruin of his hopes, anxiety not to be identified with any of his musical contemporaries, fear of the unknown but growing power of the atonal school—Stravinsky had reached the point where, with a gesture of almost light-hearted abandon, he deliberately turned his back on his own intrinsic talents.

There is a kind of sacrilege in rejecting the heritage of the past in this summary fashion. It is like abjuring one's faith in order to embrace the cult of strange gods. Henceforth Stravinsky's new works have to be judged in the light of the question—what are the musical results of his solemn and thorough-going renunciation?

A MUSICAL CARICATURE

His aesthetic conversion first made itself apparent in a rather indirect fashion—by his denial of the five Russian composers who had formed the Group of Five, particularly his old master Rimsky-Korsakov, and by an unexpected outburst of enthusiasm for Tchaikovsky who being admittedly the most Germanic of the Russian composers, had the closest links with Western Europe. For French musicians, it is difficult to understand how the hypersensitivity and indecisiveness of the composer of *Swan Lake* and the Pathetic Symphony could arouse the sympathy of an anti-romantic like Stravinsky, unless it was due to some kind of a whim or paradox. Perhaps the answer is a simple one, and it is to be attributed to the attraction of opposites. It is also possible that because of his opposition to the folk music of the Group of Five Tchaikovsky provided Stravinsky with a link which enabled him, while breaking with the Russia of today, to preserve a link with the Russia of yesterday.

Diaghilev must have been faced with a similar problem when he asked his friend to revise the orchestration of Tchaikovsky's ballet *The Sleeping Beauty*. This step led to the composition of *Mavra*. Here through the choice of subject which was inspired by Pushkin's story 'The Little House in Kolomna' Stravinsky assumed (as he himself was not slow to point out) an attitude opposed to the Five and on the side of Tchaikovsky; and in doing so he was merely continuing on the route he had already taken when he wrote *Pulcinella*—the abandonment of national Russian elements in his music in an attempt to forge a style that would be universally acceptable.

The action of *Mavra* takes place in a little Russian town in the middle of the nineteenth century. The setting shows a middle-class interior with old-fashioned furniture—a clock under a glass cover in the centre of the mantelpiece, ancestors' portraits on the walls, padded chairs—the whole room evocative of the period of Charles X. There are four characters: the lively Parasha, daughter of the house; her mother who is a chatterbox and a miser; the Hussar, a provincial Don Juan, who is wooing Parasha; and a neighbour, who likes joining the mother for a friendly gossip. The action deals with ordinary household affairs and is very compact.

The household is all at sea since the death of its dear old devoted servant—*She was a nigger for work!*—and just at that moment the cost of everything seems to rise. Parasha goes off to find a new servant, who will be content with a comparatively modest wage, and returns with a fine strong girl, who answers to the name of Mavra, but is none other than the Hussar in disguise. By this ingenious stratagem Parasha hopes to keep her flighty suitor close at hand. But left alone in the house, the Hussar unfortunately decides it's time he had a shave. Mother and daughter return unexpectedly. The mother is scandalised; the Hussar tries to escape; the neighbour rushes in; and the curtain falls on a scene of general confusion.

In setting this amusing little plot, the composer aimed at making a caricature of a musical form. This was a different process from the farce that he had produced in *Reynard* where he treated the anecdotal side of the fable as something quite distinct from the musical score. Just as Picasso, at a certain moment of his career, had had the idea of assembling on his canvas heterogeneous objects of common origin—fragments of newspaper, pieces of cloth, bits of packing paper—so Stravinsky took over certain features from nineteenth-century opera such as the vamped accompaniment, vocal turns, cadences etc. and used them as material for a musical burlesque, allowing various contrapuntal devices to upset the traditional warp of harmony. One is reminded of those street singers who, oblivious of the need for careful adjustment between the vocal line and accompaniment, involuntarily lapse into harmonic confusion and obtain as ludicrous an effect as if a person were to wear a dinner jacket with a pair of skiing trousers. In Stravinsky's case the confusion was intentional, and that added to the sense of caricature already obtained by his continual allusions to old obsolete tricks of *bel canto*. The music has a certain verve about it, which shows that the composer enjoyed writing it and in some ways it is reminiscent of Chabrier and Satie.

But while *Mavra* because of its burlesque tendencies can be grouped with *Petrushka* and the two series of Easy Pieces for Piano Duet, and even with the *Pribaoutki*, it is far from sharing the same characteristics as these works. In essence, it is different. Instead of the spontaneous wit and truculence that fused so amicably in the score of *Petrushka*, there has been substituted an intellectual approach that leads to all the stylistic nonsense and knowing tricks of writing that make the score of *Mavra* amuse the technicians and professional musicians, but bathetic where ordinary members of the audience are concerned. In any case, this luke-warm confection did not meet with much approval; and I remember that at the time of its first performance a little satirical quip was current 'Ce *Mavra*, c'est vraiment mavrant!'* But perhaps that is to treat rather too lightly a work that Stravinsky looks on as forming a turning point in his musical career.

*'This *Mavra*'s really most distressing!'

'Reynard': set by Larionov

Design by Larionov for Reynard

AN ERROR OF CHRONOLOGICAL PERSPECTIVE

Unfortunately the public, owing to an error of chronological perspective, was unable to understand that *Mavra* represented a turning point in Stravinsky's style. The Russian Ballet posters announcing the first performance on 3rd June, 1922, of the double bill of *Reynard* and *Mavra* helped to propagate this confusion; and the position was made worse the following year when Diaghilev's company produced *The Wedding*. Few of the audience read their programmes carefully enough to realise that the new ballet that was being presented was really at least five years old and had been conceived and composed in a very different atmosphere from the Paris of 1923. The more circumspect might look on the score as another success scored by the composer of *Petrushka*: but Stravinsky himself had reached the point where he was beginning to profess indifference to his earlier works.

In fact, it had needed all Diaghilev's influence as a friend to persuade him to find a solution to the problem that had been worrying him for so many years—how to instrument the score of *The Wedding* so as to eradicate the overblown magic of the full orchestra that Cocteau had so vehemently denounced in the music of Wagner and Debussy, and even in *The Rite of Spring*. A 'black and white' orchestra—the percussive effect of four pianos augmented by a large group of percussion instruments providing a violent contrast with the sostenuto style of the singing—this was Stravinsky's solution and the way he found of exorcising the spell of the full orchestra. The ballet was produced in a very simple setting by Natalia Goncharova with choreography of great nobility devised by Nijinska. It was universally greeted as a masterpiece; and this judgment has stood the test of time. Stravinsky's admirers, happy to recognise the score of *The Wedding* as a kindred utterance to that of his early ballets, decided that *Mavra* had better be regarded as a work to be ignored. The result was that the emergence of the new Stravinsky was hardly noticed at all, since everyone was still dazzled by the glory of the old.

'RETURN TO BACH'

The 'pure music' compositions that followed and helped to focus public attention on this new aspect of Stravinsky as a musician, particularly the first three of them, showed a marked tendency towards strict counterpoint. This recalled the style and manner of the great Cantor sufficiently closely to justify the musical slogan that was current in the early 1920s of a 'return to Bach'. The Octet of 1923, the Concerto for Piano and Wind Orchestra (1924) and the Sonata and Serenade for piano solo (written in 1924 and 1925 respectively) revealed Stravinsky's tendency to adopt a neoclassical style characterised by the use of the same rhythmic principle that had already appeared in *The Wedding* (but in a different polyphonic context) and had been borrowed from the Brandenburg Concertos, *viz.* the uninterrupted regular flow of quavers or semiquavers arranged in varied patterns. On the other hand, polytonality tended to disappear without leaving behind any trace of the cubist devices of *Mavra*. It is to be noted that in trying to adapt his musical thought to the models of the past, Stravinsky showed himself increasingly susceptible to the gravitational forces of tonality—that miniature solar system—and at first that attraction made itself manifest mainly on the architectonic level.

This new style, which ran counter to the general musical tendency of the period, found its climax in the Piano Concerto, a work of much greater stature and richer polyphony than the other three.

The *Serenade*, which he wrote on returning from his first trip to the United States, was more closely related to the Italian masters than to Bach, because of its use of rather obvious arpeggio figurations and (in the second movement, Romanza) of an ornate melodic line derived from coloratura vocal writing. This work showed his susceptibility to Italian influences, and though their effect might be gay and sprightly, they also brought with them the dangers of slackness and slickness.

On reflection it seems that Stravinsky's 'return to Bach' did not last long. Other models were soon to be brought into service, while tonality was to exercise an increasingly strong pull on the melodic structure of his music.

Supposed portrait of Stravinsky by Paul Klee, 1923

CONDUCTOR AND VIRTUOSO

Stravinsky's career as conductor and virtuoso dates from the spring of 1921, when he conducted *Petrushka* at the Teatro Real, Madrid, in the presence of Alfonso XIII, his Queen and the Queen-Mother. After this, he toured Spain, Belgium, Holland, Switzerland and Germany, and his fame as a conductor started to grow.

He has given an amusing account of his début as concert pianist on 22nd May, 1924, at a Koussevitzky Concert at the Paris Opera House. He was so nervous that at the moment when he was about to launch into the Largo of his Piano Concerto, he suddenly realised he had completely forgotten how it opened. He cast an anxious glance in the direction of the conductor who helped to restore his memory by whistling the first notes of the theme. His nervousness as an executant continued for many years; and I can remember an occasion when I was conducting a concert at the Salle Pleyel in 1934 and he had a similar lapse of memory in playing the cadenza in his *Capriccio*—a slip that caused me considerable anxiety at the time.

It is easy to imagine the interest shown by the public at the prospect of hearing—and seeing—Stravinsky play one of his own compositions. He naturally took his début as a concert pianist with complete seriousness; and it seemed prudent that his public appearance at the Koussevitzky Concert should be preceded by a kind of private 'dress rehearsal'. This was organised by his friend and supporter, the Princess Edmond de Polignac, in her private house. This cultured woman who had been Miss Singer before her marriage, showed great interest in the arts as a young girl; and in her memoirs* she recalls how when she was asked how she would like to celebrate her fourteenth birthday, she chose a performance of Beethoven's 14th Quartet, which at that time was considered to be so advanced as to be more or less unintelligible. Her taste for painting led her to work in the studios of Félix Barrias in the rue de Bruxelles, and of Thomas Couture, who had been Manet's master. But the dark bituminous tones and ochre yellows then in fashion were distasteful to her, and she was soon dubbed an eccentric by her family because of her admiration for the artists of the open-air school—Monet, Sisley, and Manet among others, all of whom belonged to the honourable ranks of artists whose paintings were rejected by officialdom.

After her marriage, Paris became her favourite place of residence; but it was at Villerville, near Trouville, where at that time a small colony of painters and musicians used to spend the summer, that she first encountered Gabriel Fauré, then a young man of twenty-eight. She made it clear that she greatly admired his work; and the *Mélodies de Venise*, were in fact composed at Villerville and are a memento of a visit he paid her in 1890. Unfortunately, to her great disappointment, these pieces were written, not as she had hoped, in the exquisite little salon she had prepared for him in her charming Renaissance house of San-Gregorio, but on a vulgar marble-topped table in the Café Florian.

And so the Princess's memoirs are peopled, not only with great artists and literary figures, but also with a whole cluster of distinguished musicians including Ravel, Debussy, de Falla, Erik Satie and Reynaldo Hahn. The last of these ended by getting bored with her soirées, because

*Memoirs of the late Princess Edmond de Polignac, *Horizon*, August 1945.

he violently disapproved of the *avant garde* tendency of the music presented there; and it is certainly difficult to understand how this composer, considered by some to be the spiritual heir of Théodore Dubois and Massenet, could stomach the music of Stravinsky who, since 1919, had been one of the chief attractions of her salon in the Avenue Henri-Martin.

Before the private dress rehearsal of the Piano Concerto (at which Jean Wiener played the second piano part), preliminary performances of *Mavra, Reynard, The Wedding,* and *The Soldier's Tale* had been offered the Princess's guests in private audition; and she had also underwritten the cost of *Mavra* and *Reynard,* when these two works were produced by Diaghilev's Russian Ballet. Subsequently, this splendid series of private auditions was completed by performances of the Piano Sonata and *Oedipus Rex.*

Stravinsky's reputation rapidly spread and grew, from private soirées to public performances, from Paris to most of the other European towns of musical importance; and in 1925 he became a figure of world importance as the result of a triumphal tour of the United States. But such success could be obtained only after a considerable struggle; and of his three related activities, it was that of conductor that was perhaps the hardest for him to master. The rhythmic complexity of his music—especially in his earlier scores—confronted him with a number of difficult technical problems to solve, for the least error in beating the irregular series of compound metres inevitably produced confusion, if not catastrophe.

It is easy to understand the difficulties experienced by Stravinsky, despite his considerable talent, in embarking on this new career as a conductor. Sometimes these led to his demanding an unusual number of rehearsals; and it may be thought that they were also the indirect cause of his gradual renunciation of the rich rhythmic complexities that had been taken for granted in earlier works like *The Rite of Spring, The Wedding* and *The Soldier's Tale.* Perhaps the composer's change of attitude and adoption of the qualities of ease and facility as guiding attributes of his music allowed the conductor to recover that freedom of movement and gesture that Karsavina had already noted as characteristic of the young Stravinsky in St. Petersburg when he played through the newly completed score of *The Fire Bird* at the piano.

Stravinsky and the Princess de Polignac

OEDIPUS REX, OR THE COMPOSER AT THE CROSS ROADS

Having spent about three years, from the Octet to the Serenade, in elaborating the elements of his new musical language, Stravinsky now had the wish to apply it to a dramatic work. Perhaps he intended to provide a contrast, whether opera or oratorio, to the lightweight satire of *Mavra*, the last of his scores to be written for the theatre. The main problem, with which he was intensely preoccupied, was how to ensure that even in the theatre the audience's attention should be concentrated almost exclusively on the music. And he decided that the best way to prevent their attention from straying down the byways of the plot was to choose some universally familiar subject. He discussed this project with his friend Jean Cocteau; and the choice of the collaborators fell on one of the most striking classical tragedies—that of Oedipus, who had been engaged in an unconscious contest with those supernatural powers that 'are always watching us from a world beyond the

Stravinsky and Cocteau at a revival of 'Oedipus Rex'

gates of death'. Such was the genesis of *Oedipus Rex*, another milestone in Stravinsky's musical development.

This is an extremely curious work. On the one hand, it is closely related to opera because it has a spectacular side, including costumes and scenery, which indicate the period and place of the action. On the other, it breaks away from the usual notions of time and place by introducing the sort of character that is usually found in oratorio, *viz*. a reciter. It is most unusual to have the action of a stage spectacle broken by the appearance of a speaker wearing a dark suit, who looks as if he had strayed from the concert platform and speaks to the audience like a lecturer—for that is Cocteau's intention—summarising the plot with a flat inexpressive voice, and outlining the scenes that are about to be presented by the singers. The appearance of this speaker represents the intrusion of contemporaneity into the action of a distant epoch; and this gives rise to an anachronism which would have daunted most authors. But Cocteau and Stravinsky were sufficiently subtle to know how to exploit this device in order to achieve a thoroughly unrealistic effect. The scenery was to be constructed so as to avoid depth. The main protagonists—Oedipus, Jocasta and Creon—were to appear like living statues, with built-up costumes, which allowed them only restricted head- and hand-movments. Finally, the characters were to express themselves in a dead tongue—Latin—since Stravinsky's view was that 'a special language, and not that of current converse, was required for subjects touching on the sublime'. And it should be added that in setting this Latin text he was able to indulge his desire to free himself both from the literal domination of the word and also from the demands of prosody.

A setting without perspective, static actors, an esoteric language, co-existence of two widely separated periods—these are the essential features of this 'opera-oratorio', which is like an archaic bas-relief thrown up in our modern age. The music expresses this conception through its careful formal construction, making considerable use of symmetry, and evoking the spirit of Sophocles through that of Handel; and in this it reminds one of the similar step taken by Picasso a few years previously when he had signalled his own return to the antique in a series of paintings of men and women with Greek features, and classical nudes of gigantic proportions.

While it cannot be denied that in its monumental proportions, this opera-oratorio recaptures something of classical grandeur, it is no less true that from the musical point of view, this grandeur—like a strong-hold of harmonic conformity against which the waves of living music break in vain—seems to be immobilised in a past tense; and this feeling of coagulation is all the more apparent when the score is compared with those of two younger French composers: the Aeschylean trilogy (*Agamemnon*, *The Libation-Bearers* and *The Eumenides*) set by Darius Milhaud between 1913 and 1922, and the *Antigone* that Arthur Honegger finished in 1927, the same year as the first performance of *Oedipus Rex*. Without examining these scores in detail—which would be outside the scope of the present volume—it is difficult not to be struck by the contrast they offer with Stravinsky's work. Although Milhaud's *Oresteia* cannot really be compared with Honegger's *Antigone*, they both have this characteristic in common—the novelty of their musical idiom definitely situates them in the period in which they were composed. Neither Milhaud nor Honegger felt any need to have recourse to one of the musical idioms of the past in order to treat an antique subject. They did what Beethoven and Handel did in their own time, by clothing their thoughts in their own musical language, and not that of anyone else. Were they wrong? Did their action harm the art of music? Certainly not. It may reasonably be asked, which of these three—Milhaud, Honegger or Stravinsky—each of whom was confronted by the problem of setting a Greek tragedy, whose subject (let it not be forgotten) was actual at the time it was written, has been the most faithful interpreter of the original? Which of these three really acted in conformity with the precept that was to be enunciated a few years later in *Poetics of Music*—'*we have a single duty towards music, namely, to invent it*'.

In the course of their collaboration, Cocteau and Stravinsky decided to offer their work as an act of homage to Diaghilev on the occasion of the celebration of the twentieth anniversary of his theatrical activity in the spring of 1927. They wanted to give him a surprise; but in order to keep their secret till the last moment, they were constrained to produce the work, not in its stage form, but as an oratorio. This was a mistake. Sandwiched between two ballets which were mounted with all the usual brilliance of the Russian Ballet which was appearing at the Théâtre Sarah-Bernhardt that season, *Oedipus Rex* seemed like an intruder on the scene and disconcerted a public that had come to enjoy the dancers' points and *entrechats*. Its glacial reception was entirely undeserved for, despite the academic turn of its musical idiom, the work is most impressive and crowns the period of composition inaugurated by the Ingres-like *Pulcinella* with classical glory.

Since the end of the first World War, the musical life of Europe had revived in all its vigour. First, Paris was its centre. Later it spread over Central Europe, and Berlin gradually became a strong-point. So it was not altogether unexpected that the first performance of *Oedipus Rex* as an opera should have taken place at the Krolloper, Berlin, in February, 1928.

A new concert public was being formed in Paris—very different from the public of the old series of Sunday concerts—and it frequented the brilliant gala performances that Koussevitzky gave first at the Opera House and later at the Théâtre des Champs-Elysées which had also become the setting of the Concerts Straram. New composers appeared, grouped round Richard Strauss in Germany and Maurice

Ravel in France. Schoenberg, Bartok, Hindemith and Alban Berg were growing up in rivalry with the youthful masters of the French School— Arthur Honegger, Darius Milhaud, Georges Auric, Francis Poulenc, Albert Roussel. In this international field, a new work by Stravinsky was always listened to with curiosity. But the new direction taken by his music could not fail to disconcert a number of people; and there were many admirers of works like *The Rite of Spring*, *The Wedding*, and *Reynard* who could not stand *Oedipus Rex*. Ill-natured attacks were directed against him, such as the second number (*Vielseitigkeit*) of *Drei Satirem* (op. 28) where the text as well as the music was written by Schoenberg:—

> *Ja, wer tommerlt denn da?*
> *Das ist ja der kleine Modernsky!*
> *Hat sich ein Bubikopf schneiden lassen;*
> *sieht ganz gut aus!*
> *Wie echt falsches Haar!*
> *Wie eine Perücke!*
> *Ganz (wie sich ihn der kleine Modernsky vorstellt),*
> *Ganz der Papa Bach!*
> (But who's this beating the drum?
> It's little Modernsky!
> He's had his hair cut in an old-fashioned queue,
> And it looks quite nice,
> Like real false hair—
> Like a wig—
> Just like (at least little Modernsky thinks so)
> Just like Father Bach!

Setting for 'Oedipus Rex' designed by Dülberg, Berlin, 1928 ▲

Doubtless this caricature should not be taken literally as being the expression of a widely-held opinion. Nevertheless, some of Stravinsky's friends also showed considerable disappointment, although they expressed it in less acid terms.

Ramuz, for example, who continued to live in quiet proximity to the peasants in the Canton of Vaud, now saw with disquietude the companion of earlier years, who during the war period had shared with him so many ideas and thoughts and work projects, caught up into the superficial whirlpool of Paris society. Continually on the move, visiting all the major towns of Europe and America, Stravinsky had become a world celebrity. His name was news. In this new figure, Ramuz failed to recognise his former friend, or even to understand him. Referring affectionately to the score of *The Wedding* on which as translator he had lavished so much care, he addressed Stravinsky with a note of sadness in his voice:—'Perhaps today you feel inclined to disapprove of this music's impulsiveness, or apparent lack of discipline, or its sense of the picturesque: now that you have more or less completely sworn allegiance to Apollo, you find fault with those qualities that it may owe to Dionysos.' Doubtless these words betray a feeling of personal disappointment: but it is difficult not to recognise in them some of the dominant characteristics of the new Stravinsky.

While for some time—and particularly since the composition of *Oedipus Rex*—Stravinsky had put himself forward as the defender of law and order and tradition, he had also expressed a number of paradoxical opinions on the music of the past, refusing to allow Beethoven, for example, the gift of melody which he found to be the natural quality of Bellini's music, and maintaining that Verdi's earlier and obviously weaker operas such as *Rigoletto* and *La Traviata* were superior to his masterpiece *Falstaff*. Of his contemporaries and their work, he said little in his *Chronicle*. He might mention Prokofiev and Hindemith, but he had nothing to say about Berg's *Wozzeck*, which had received its first performance in Berlin in 1925, the year in which he had produced his Italianate *Serenade*.

His attitude has rather resembled that of Cocteau and Picasso in his secret desire to surprise and disconcert his audience and go against the stream of current opinion in order subsequently to recapture the lead; but it would be unfair to interpret only in this way the extreme mobility of spirit that has characterised these three artists. They are always anxious to have a problem to solve; and in the case of Picasso, he has frequently had occasion to work simultaneously on several different canvases in several different styles.

After making allowance for the inherent difference between the executive methods of a painter and composer, a similar diversity is to be found in Stravinsky, with the result that sometimes one of his works, or a group of compositions, seems unexpectedly to run counter to another group, whereas in reality the opposing works are comple-

Florence, 1925 (Coll. Th. Stravinsky)

mentary and complete each other. And this observation has particular force at a moment when one is about to explore the three different pathways that radiate from the cross-roads of *Oedipus Rex, viz*. the baroque, the hieratic and the classical.

(*From left to right*) Max Jacob, Auric, Stravinsky, Cocteau, Poulenc, Milhaud, Picasso

THE BAROQUE

The first work belonging to the baroque group was *Apollo Musagetes*, which claimed to be the precursor of a melodic revival. This *ballet blanc* in classical style conformed to the plan of a suite, made up of solo dance variations, *pas de deux* and *pas d'action*. It was followed the same year (1928) by another ballet score, *The Fairy's Kiss*, which used Tchaikovsky as a pretence for reviving sentimental romanticism. In both these works, as also in *A Card Game* of 1936 which features a quotation from Rossini's *The Barber of Seville*, the music shows the ill effects of the Italian influence of the music of Bellini and Donizetti, with their tendency towards flabby texture and inflated line. Unfortunately their degenerate baroque style, with its false abundance and false charm was fashionable in France in the nineteenth century; but it was strongly resisted by Fauré, Debussy, Ravel and Roussel, who helped to get the offending works removed to the attics of the imaginary musical museum of the present century.

Diaghilev, 1924

Does this imply that all Stravinsky's baroque works should be condemned? Certainly not, for between *The Fairy's Kiss* and *A Card Game* came a number of other baroque works of undoubted value. For instance in 1931 he wrote the Concerto in D for violin and orchestra, which had been commissioned by his publishers, Messrs. Schott, for the violinist Samuel Dushkin. In this, the rhythmic structure gave the impression of having been written by a J. S. Bach who was familiar with, and enjoyed, the disarticulated syncopations of jazz. The following year Stravinsky was even more successful with the *Duo Concertante*, which was also written for Dushkin. Here he showed that thanks to his close co-operation with Dushkin, who had helped him to obtain a mastery of the transcendental technique of the violin, he was now in a position fully to realise his aim of creating a work of musical versification inspired by the bucolic poets of antiquity. A restrained lyricism informs the whole work, especially the first Eclogue, where violin and piano interlace their serene cantilenas, and the Gigue with its engagingly fresh and sprightly air.

As for the *Capriccio* for piano and orchestra of 1929, it is undoubtedly the masterpiece of this baroque group. With its intense dynamism, it combines a wealth of unexpected fantasy, and its resourceful pianistic writing is derived from the same source that inspired Carl Maria Weber.

Design by Theodor Stravinsky

THE HIERATIC

Turning from the baroque works already mentioned, Stravinsky set off in another direction, one which so far he had scarcely explored, and this led to the composition of two of his masterpieces— *The Symphony of Psalms* which followed the *Capriccio* in 1930, and *Persephone* which was written immediately after the *Duo Concertante* in 1933. In both works, the features of the Russian composer reappeared behind the new mask of the western European composer, bringing to light, like buried but unforgotten treasure, the love of modality that he had seemed to abandon after raising his monument in sound to the memory of Debussy in 1920.

The *Symphony of Psalms* gives the impression of being inspired by a harsh, strong feeling that has come from the remote past, a tremendous wave of hope that has grown out of the anguish of mankind, punctuated by occasional lightning flashes revealing the countenance of Jehovah; and in this it recalls the hieratic element that was present in Stravinsky's setting of one of the two Verlaine poems that he composed at the time of *The Fire Bird*.

The same hieratic quality links this religious musical masterpiece with another work of outstanding importance, the pagan *Persephone* commissioned by Ida Rubenstein for her 1934 season at the Paris Opera House. The ideal that this famous dancer set herself at the outset of her career was to revive the harmonious triad of Poetry, Music and Dance that were the basic ingredients of the classical Greek Theatre. To bring back Poetry to rejoin the arts of Music and Dance would complete the work already initiated by Diaghilev through the Russian Ballet. The *Martyrdom of St. Sebastian* (1911) was the first step towards the realisation of her aims; and in this as well as her many subsequent roles she succeeded in evoking not only a figure of flesh and blood but also the spirit that animated the being.

She was perhaps especially successful in the character of Persephone, for in André Gide's poem the daughter of Demeter is not, as in certain other versions of the myth, forcibly ravished by the powers of darkness, but decides of her own free will to go down to Hades to visit the kingdom of the dead. '*On fields strewn with asphodel I see an entire people wandering, bereft of hope.*' What could have been more appropriate than to cast for this role of a character who in Gide's poem is actuated by feelings of pity that seem almost Christian in their intensity, someone who during the whole of her life had quietly, almost surreptitiously, done all that was in her power to lighten the sufferings of others? Soldiers who had been wounded in the first World War, unfortunate souls who had crept away into a corner to hide their poverty and distress, musicians racked by despair because of some unforeseen disaster, all alike were recipients of Ida Rubinstein's charity.—'*Nymphs, my sisters, my beloved companions, how can I live henceforth, how can I laugh and sing my carefree songs, now that I've seen and know that a whole people lives in discontent and suffers while it waits?*'

Stravinsky treated this myth with all the intensity appropriate for a hymn to universal pity and all the religious feeling needed to portray a rite pertaining to the ancient orphic mysteries. I had the pleasure of helping him to prepare the vocal score, and to my mind there is no doubt that the noble invocations of Eumolpus, the choruses of the nymphs and shades, and the numerous passages for mime are among his finest pages.

THE CLASSICAL

Right at the beginning of the pathway leading in the direction of classicism stands the Concerto for Two Solo Pianos. Its pianistic technique, with its systematic use of repeated notes, seems to be derived from the cymbalom whose metallic timbre had haunted Stravinsky for a number of years. This concerto has an extraordinary polyphonic intensity which is worked up to an impressive climax in the final fugue where the subject is developed in various ways, including a passage in retrograde motion, and a coda in which the subject is inverted. Here, Stravinsky's classical style reaches a point where it seems to achieve a successful synthesis of elements drawn from the major keyboard works of Bach and Beethoven.

In the shadow of such a masterpiece, the *Dumbarton Oaks Concerto* (1938), named after the property of Mr. and Mrs. Bliss who commissioned it, and the Symphony in C (begun in 1938 and finished two years later) seem built to a more modest scale. While the style of the former work is at times almost academic, in the Symphony Stravinsky made a bold attempt to renew the conception of symphonic form as originally developed by Stamitz, Haydn and Mozart.

RETROSPECT

While exploring the three main avenues of Stravinsky's artistic creation that radiate from the symbolical cross roads of *Oedipus Rex*, an event has been overlooked that caused Stravinsky great grief at the time—Diaghilev's death from diabetes at Venice on 19th August, 1929. For twenty years the great impresario had devoted his energy and skill to building up a ballet company which had been the vehicle for displaying the talents of a whole generation of artists, dancers, painters, designers, and composers. Stravinsky had been one of Diaghilev's earliest collaborators and by his death he lost not only a patron and a friend with whom he delighted to argue, but also the advantage of having in the Russian Ballet a company that was always ready to mount his latest theatrical score. *Apollo Musagetes*, produced at the Théâtre Sarah-Bernhardt in 1928, was the last work of his to be produced by the Russian Ballet, and the company did not survive Diaghilev's death.

In 1937, the year in which French music lost two of its great exponents—Albert Roussel and Maurice Ravel—Stravinsky celebrated his 55th birthday. His threefold activity as composer, conductor and pianist had led him to carry out extensive tours in North and South America as well as Europe. His son, Soulima, had made his début as a concert pianist first at Barcelona and then at Paris in the *Capriccio* and Piano Concerto with his father at the conductor's pult; and subsequently he joined his father as the second soloist in the Concerto for Two Solo Pianos during a tour of South America in 1935.

Since 1920 Stravinsky's attachment to France had deepened. He had set up his residence first at Garches, and subsequent moves had brought him to Biarritz, Nice and Voreppe. In 1936 he became naturalised and was an unsuccessful candidate for election to the Académie des Beaux-Arts, Florent Schmitt, composer of the cyclopean Psalm XLVI, being elected in his place. At the same time, he had for some years been under contract to the Columbia Recording Company, and this had served to strengthen his ties with the United States.

Towards the end of the thirties the international political situation clouded over, and there seemed to be imminent danger of war. The composition of the Symphony in C was started in France in the year of Munich, but its completion was delayed by the outbreak of hostilities. Invited in the autumn of 1939 by Harvard University to deliver a series of lectures on the Poetics of Music, Stravinsky left France immediately, and when the lecture series was completed, decided not to return, but to settle in America.

A Igor Stravinsky
en souvenir de "l'Oiseau
Marc Chagall 1949 Paris de Feu"

*Drawing reprinted from 'Stravinsky' (edited by Merle Armitage) New York,
Duell, Sloan, Pierce*

Hollywood

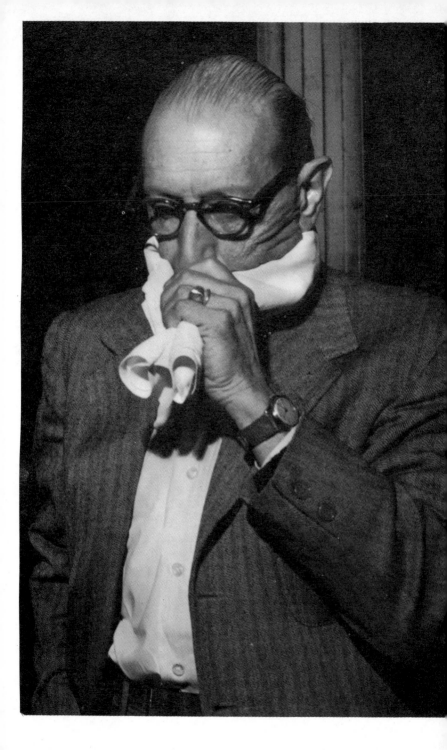

Hollywood

After the Harvard lectures, Stravinsky left the East Coast and found a house on the outskirts of Hollywood, California. This part of the United States has an agreeably temperate climate like that of the French Riviera, and the light is of limpid clarity. Here, far removed from the bustle and tumult of the great American industrial towns and also from the war which was being waged with savage intensity in Europe, he was free to lead a comparatively calm life, almost like that of a monk, with a minutely regulated time-table. After a quarter of an hour's session devoted early each morning to Hungarian calisthenics, he would spend the rest of the morning in composition. Lunch would be served at two o'clock sharp; and afterwards he would enjoy a game of Chinese chequers. This has always been one of his favourite pastimes, and he refuses to forego his postprandial game, even when travelling or visiting friends. He is devoted to it and does not enjoy being beaten. He pays special attention to the garden where the flowers encouraged by the favourable climate grow in profusion, and also to the pet birds housed in a large cage near the dining room. The rest of the day is taken up with score reading, private and business correspondence (usually very heavy), orchestration, and the correction of proofs.

Sound-proofed and carefully isolated from the rest of the house, his study is similar to the one he used at Morges. The only difference is that there are more manuscripts, papers and business documents in the drawers, all carefully labelled and filed, and more personal mementoes on the walls in the shape of pictures and drawings by Picasso, Fernand Leger, and his son Theodore. As formerly, his table is covered with a great variety of objects—the tools of composition—and this makes it look more like a work bench than a desk. This sparsely furnished room also contains two pianos—one a grand, and the other a muffled upright.

This is the setting where with intermittent regularity his new works are conceived and brought to life; and their amazing diversity reflects the workings of a mind continuously preoccupied with a quest for novelty and change, and interested in every aspect of the science of music. Faced by a request for a piece for a circus, or a jazz band, or a musical revue, he immediately finds his appetite for composition whetted by the new problems to be tackled; and by dint of the technical mastery he has built up over so many years, he is able to solve them as easily as he writes out a cheque.

METAMORPHOSES

Is it possible to divide Stravinsky's prolific and protean output into
the three main divisions suggested above and find in his multifarious
musical thoughts the essence of these different orders? In aesthetics it is
always dangerous to try to erect a closed system; but it is sometimes
helpful to try to bring order out of confusion. It should not be forgotten,
however, that no one of these three aspects of the composer's art can be
safely neglected; and at the same time no one aspect implies an *a priori*
judgment of the other two, although the hieratic works—or, what
amounts to the same thing, the primitive works—all show a strong
tonal foundation, from which they derive special vitality.

Perhaps the roots of his classicism are not very deep. Such a suspicion
would be confirmed by the rather dull Sonata for Two Pianos, the
rather livelier *Danses Concertantes*, and the *Elegy* for solo viola, even
though the last composition owes its inspiration to Bach's sonatas for
solo violin. All these three works, however, are thrown into the shade
by the Symphony in Three Movements, which is a splendid example of
his classical manner at its best.

Feuille de propagande des Comiques, Paul Klee, 1938 (Louise Leiris Gallery)

Should one be tempted to rate his baroque works less high, when they include the *Ode* and *The Rake's Progress*? But it must be admitted that this category includes a modest group of minor works, the result of his unfortunately yielding to solicitations from various commercial enterprises whose sole object was to exploit the prestige to be gained from his name. Little need be said about the two compositions of 'symphonic jazz': the *Scherzo à la Russe* (1944) written for Paul Whiteman, who created this bastard genre, which pretends to be derived from Negro Spirituals, whereas in reality it is no more than an abominable parody of them; and the *Ebony Concerto* (1945) intended to display Woody Herman and his boys to the best advantage. As for the *Scènes de Ballet*, which was meant to form part of one of Billy Rose's Broadway revues, it is a pity that the score is so perfectly suited to the bombastic style of this type of show business. It might even be said that movements like the Variations, the passages of pantomime, and the Pas de Deux are haunted by the ghost of Aubrey Beardsley, whose influence Stravinsky thought at one time he had detected in the text of Schoenberg's *Pierrot Lunaire*. It is better to say nothing about the *Four Norwegian Moods*, where the treatment of the folksong themes shows no attempt to transform them.

Although it seems deplorable that Stravinsky's *oeuvre* should include such pot-boilers, an exception must be made in favour of the *Circus Polka*. Commissioned in 1942 by the famous Barnum and Bailey Circus as a dance for their team of elephants, the work triumphs because of its gay modulations, the droll quotation of a passage from Schubert's Marche Militaire, and the composer's indefatigable playfulness. *Spiritus ubi vult spirat . . .*'

EPITAPH

The death of Natalie Koussevitzky, who with her husband had been one of the founders of the music publishing house, Edition Russe de Musique, struck Stravinsky with a sense of personal loss. Since 1909 when Serge Koussevitzky had welcomed the young composer with his score of the opening act of *The Nightingale*, the relation between the two families had been one of close friendship; and from the beginning both Serge and Natalie had taken an active part in propagating the music of their compatriot.

Serge Koussevitzky, who has already been mentioned in connection with the musical life of Paris, was a remarkable man. At an early age he was a virtuoso executant and succeeded in making a reputation for himself as a solo double-bass player before becoming one of the best known conductors of international fame. For about a quarter of a century his firm had the almost exclusive right of publishing Stravinsky's works. He was also one of the greatest interpreters of Stravinsky's music. Furthermore, to him was due the honour of commissioning the Symphony of Psalms, which was written to celebrate the fiftieth anniversary of the Boston Symphony Orchestra which he had conducted since 1924.

In the *Ode*, an elegiacal chant dedicated to Natalie's memory, the first part (Eulogy) after a mysterious introduction on trumpets and horns which recalls the magic of *The Rite of Spring* develops a musical phrase, which by virtue of its romantic contour and the pianistic form of its repeated note accompaniment seems curiously near to Schumann, and this is taken up by the strings and then the woodwind. The baroque impression made by this intimate elegy is emphasised by the middle movement (Eclogue) with its unexpected flourishes for horns, which recall a woodland hunting scene. The concluding Epitaph written in Stravinsky's mystic vein, evokes the etherial regions of the Elysian Fields in an idiom that recalls the Symphonies of Wind Instruments. After an interval of just over twenty years, the composer found himself once more inspired by the death of a friend to write a work of piety in which the memory of the dead was enshrined with musical radiance.

BEETHOVEN REDISCOVERED

To attempt to establish a parallel between Stravinsky and Beethoven may seem unexpected and even paradoxical when one recalls the disapproval frequently expressed by the Russian composer of his illustrious German predecessor. In his *Chronicle*, Stravinsky has made clear his detestation of the *Weltschmerz* that was applied as a label to so many of Beethoven's compositions; and in the *Poetics of Music*, he reproaches him for lacking the essential gift of melody. Nevertheless, when it is remembered how in his earlier works Stravinsky frequently borrowed from folk music and later on had recourse to the use of musical models supplied by earlier composers, it may be thought it would be truer to say that Stravinsky himself has spent a considerable part of his musical life seeking the very gift of melody that (according to him) Bellini inherited 'without having even so much as asked for it'.*

The word 'melody' should be defined. Some people think that melodic richness consists in the aggregation of a large number of notes through the proliferation of ornament as is the case precisely with Bellini and other Italian opera composers of that period; but that is to forget that the primitive form of liturgical chant, with little or no ornament, is just as melodically rich but in a different sense—less brilliant, admittedly, but of finer quality in the deployment of its melodic line. When it is remembered that the first movement of Beethoven's Fifth Symphony is built up from a minute cell consisting of two tones, it will be readily understood that there are many different

*Poetics of Music, Chapter II.

conceptions of melody, and in its most perfect state it is not necessarily identical with Italianate vocalisation.

It is worth noting that the meaning of the word *melos* is a limb, and its original application to a single vocal strain was overtaken by the invention of polyphony and the development of instrumental music. The genius of Beethoven consisted precisely in his understanding of the new melodic possibilities that this opened up; and Stravinsky's suggestion that Beethoven 'spent his whole life imploring the aid of this gift which he lacked' fails to take into account Beethoven's passionate lifelong quest for the vital dynamic essence to be extracted from polyphony, which may indeed appear as melody, but can also become manifest as rhythm, chords, or even silent pauses.

Stravinsky himself showed complete awareness of this dynamic principle when he wrote his Symphony in Three Movements in 1945, a work which succeeds in revivifying the classical form of the symphony —just as in Beethoven's Fifth, most of the important themes (especially those in the first and third movements) gravitate round a strictly limited number of notes and seem thereby to accumulate a reserve of energy which is revealed by interplay between the fixed elements and the moving elements and the fascinating ambiguity that this creates.★

This important work, dedicated to the New York Philharmonic Symphony Society, forms a climax to his quest for musical form, for it is in no wise a copy or a pastiche reproducing the superficial appearance of an accepted model, but a new and original incarnation of the creative principle. I fully agree with the author of the *Poetics of Music* that this creative principle which is purely musical in essence has nothing common with *Weltschmerz* or any other manifestation of the pathetic fallacy. Fortified by its dynamic potential, it appears in all the compositions where Stravinsky renews contact with the element from which all his greatest works have sprung—the rhythmic flow that governs his music in time.

A MEDIEVAL STAINED-GLASS WINDOW

In the light of the somewhat superficial works that surround it, the *Mass* (composed between 1945 and 1947) may be looked on as an act of contrition. The austere polyphony of this score harks back to the past, and in some of its passages to an almost medieval hieraticism—as, for example, in the opening Kyrie with its succession of subtle cadences, each resembling a ray of light filtering through the darkness of a sanctuary. With its embroidered appogiaturas, the Sanctus recalls the work of some of the masters of the Ars Nova who flourished in the fifteenth century, while the ornate solos of the Gloria alternating with the responses of the choir are Byzantine in form.

★See Fred Goldbeck's article in *Contrepoints*, December 1946.

A deep faith informs this *Mass*, which together with the earlier Symphony of Psalms forms a specially important facet of Stravinsky's output. It is like a stained-glass window, whose colours are dominated by deep blues and reds, and which becomes radiant when the sunlight shines through it.

A BAROQUE ORPHEUS

Orpheus belongs to the same period as the *Mass*. This ballet in three scenes was commissioned by Lincoln Kirstein for the Ballet Society of New York, and the first performance took place in New York on 28th April, 1948, with choreography by George Balanchine.

As the composer was tempted by the nature of the subject to use some of the ancient Greek modes, its polyphony generally avoids the tonality appropriate to the major/minor convention.

Two special details concerning the instrumentation should be noted. The first is the use of brass (a general custom since Monteverdi) to describe the terrors of Tartarus. The second is the way the harp is used as the equivalent in orchestral sound of the lyre of Orpheus.

The *Pas des Furies* is particularly impressive with its strangely stumping agitation and makes an excellent foil to the following *Air de Danse* where Apollo charms the infernal powers with the strains of his lyre which is joined by the bucolic sweetness of two oboes in the style of the Italian masters of the eighteenth century. A menacing Interlude precedes the *Pas d'Action* where the Bacchantes attack Orpheus and tear him to pieces. With its panting syncopation, this dance seems to be based on the same rhythmic principle as the final movement of *The Rite of Spring*. Nevertheless, it manages to preserve its own identity. The greater part of it is written in the same subdued orchestral colours that characterise the rest of the score; but its fortissimo climax is the only instrumental tutti in the whole work, and immediately afterwards it breaks off into shuddering fragments appropriate to Apollo's dismemberment. A slow introduction and a slow coda, both in the Dorian mode, give the score a sense of symmetry, and the coda blossoms into a noble apotheosis that accompanies the resurrection of Orpheus and the appearance of Apollo.

In this work, Stravinsky succeeds (where he had so signally failed with the conventional music of *Apollo Musagetes* about 20 years before) in reanimating, in musical terms, one of the antique myths. As in the *Mass*, but to a much less intense degree, his music for *Orpheus* displays a deep-seated primitive feeling curiously mingled with a baroque sensibility. Whereas sometimes this primitive feeling is held in check by other forces, certain subjects seem by their very nature able to evoke it, and the myth of Orpheus was certainly one of these.

'THE RAKE'S PROGRESS':
A COUNTERPART TO 'MAVRA'

Stravinsky's next work, *The Rake's Progress*, marks another change of direction. It was inspired by Hogarth's well-known series of paintings which illustrate the unhappy story of a young man from the country who unexpectedly inherits a fortune and goes to London with the ambition of conquering the world of society, but once there rapidly succumbs to the attractions of low life and plunges into a career of debauchery and dissipation which eventually results in the loss of his fortune, honour and reason. From this morality, W. H. Auden 'the English Valéry' fashioned (in collaboration with Chester Kallmann) an opera libretto in three acts and nine scenes, in which the realistic subject matter was adroitly transformed by the introduction of the characters of Nick Shadow, the diabolical embodiment of evil, and the Rake himself, a strange amalgam of Don Juan, Faust and Peer Gynt.

Reiner, Balanchine, Stravinsky, Armstedt, Auden at a rehearsal of
'The Rake's Progress'

Stimulated by his fanatic dislike of the 'endless melody' and the leit-motifs that characterise Wagner's music dramas, Stravinsky aimed at resuscitating classical opera in his score. Hogarth's series of paintings based on the manners of the early part of the eighteenth century furnished a perfect excuse for having recourse to the musical conventions of the period—*da capo* airs with repeats, ensembles, choruses and *recitative secco*. In this he was reacting to the same considerations that had led him to try to revive the form of *opera buffa* when composing *Mavra*.

This was *a priori* a perfectly legitimate thing to do, for what counts in a work of art is not so much the formula adopted as the result. And here there is no doubt that Auden's libretto was a complete success. It should perhaps be pointed out that the mainspring of the action is motivated by sarcasm and derision. Anne Trulove, who personifies pure love, is no more than an episodic and rather shadowy figure. Neverthe-less, her intervention at the climax of the action is decisive, since she saves Tom Rakewell from eternal damnation. But it must be admitted that neither the dramatic content of the action nor the character of Anne herself seemed to inspire the composer: but that was hardly to be wondered at in view of his contempt for 'expression' in music. Never-theless, Mozart himself, who is generally looked on as a composer of 'pure' music, took considerable pains to exploit the pathos inherent in some of his operatic scenes (such as the entry of the statue of the Com-mendatore in *Don Giovanni*); and to evade this theatrical necessity is a sign of weakness in a composer.

One might have hoped that such musical reticence would be com-pensated for by a completely unified style; but such a style, while being capable of harmonising contrasting elements, ought to be something more than a mere collection of heterogeneous ingredients, and here it must be admitted that Stravinsky, while utilising a number of 'musical models' for his score, was not completely successful in reconciling the idioms of composers as different as Mozart, Gounod, Verdi and Gluck, who would probably have been rather embarrassed to find themselves in each other's company on this occasion. Add to this mixture a dash of Stravinsky's own pepper, and the result is not so much a classical opera as a work tending towards the multifarious variety of baroque.

The first performance of *The Rake's Progress*, which took place at the Fenice Theatre, Venice, in 1951, marked the first occasion on which Stravinsky returned to Europe since the outbreak of the second World War. The opera, which was subsequently produced in most of the main opera houses in the world, was generally welcomed more warmly by the public than the critics, the majority of whom were only tepid in their interest.

A RESOUNDING CONVERSION

Brentwood Park, near Los Angeles, which had been Arnold Schoenberg's home since 1934, was not more than ten miles from Stravinsky's Hollywood villa; but the proximity of these two composers did not encourage them to enter into friendly relations as neighbours, even though the fact that they were both exiles might have proved a point of common interest.

Perhaps this was too much to expect of two men of genius who had found themselves on opposite sides of the fence during the whole of their lives; and doubtless it was difficult to forget the bitterness that had marked the disputes of the rival groups of disciples that gathered round the two masters in the course of time. So the gap between them was unbridgable and unbridged.

But these personal feuds and rivalries are merely examples of temporary human aberrations and prove of little significance in the long run. What is of real importance here is to stress the fact that for a number of decades Schoenberg and Stravinsky had been looked on as being at the two opposite poles of contemporary music.

It has already been shown how Stravinsky's genius, which had at first tended towards a renewal of the basic material of music, subsequently veered towards a form of classicism that demanded the renunciation of his earlier conquests. Meanwhile, Schoenberg, who always remained faithful to his initial aims, had no hesitation in mid-career in abandoning all creative activity for a period of about eight years in order to use his retirement to perfect the technique needed to carry out his grand design. By 1915 he was no longer satisfied by the doctrine of suspended tonality which until then had formed the basic idiom of his compositions. He was anxious to discover a composing principle that would allow him to organise the twelve notes of the chromatic scale in a system which would be independent of the gravitional laws exercised by the system of classical tonality. This was the birth of the system of serial composition in virtue of which this Viennese composer was able to make the proud boast that 'German music would maintain world supremacy during the next century'.★

It is difficult to formulate a dispassionate judgment as to the value of the serial system as such; but what is significant is that for thirty-five years or more it has fertilised the compositions not only of Schoenberg himself but also of his disciples, particularly the entire work of Anton Webern and the greater part of Alban Berg's. It has also been recognised by a number of musical academies and schools in different parts of the world such as America, Germany, Switzerland etc.

In the spring of 1951 the first performance of 'The Dance Before the Golden Calf', took place at Darmstadt under Hermann Scherchen's direction. This was a fragment from the opera *Moses und Aron* on

★ *Schoenberg* by H. H. Stuckenschmidt.

which Schoenberg had been working for many years and for which he had written the libretto. News of its triumphal reception reached the master while he was ill and confined to his bed. In fact, this was one of the last successes he lived to enjoy, for a few months later on 13th July, shortly before midnight, he died, leaving this great work of his, a parable of the struggle between idealism and reality, unfinished. At the same moment Stravinsky was putting the last touches to the instrumentation of his score of *The Rake's Progress*.

At that moment the two rival composers were firmly entrenched in such opposing positions that it seemed extremely unlikely that they would ever be reconciled. Nevertheless, from 1952—that is to say, shortly after Schoenberg's death—Stravinsky began to show signs of preoccupation with the elements of serialism. In the Gigue of his Septet he placed against each instrumental entry a row of eight notes which made it clear that he had constructed this movement according to principles other than those based on traditional modes and scales, though at this point he was far from using a real dodecaphonic series.

His serial tendency became clearer and more developed in the Dirge-Canons and Song *In Memoriam Dylan Thomas* written in 1954; and it would be true to say that from that moment he made increasing use of the Schoenbergian serial system, which until then he had ignored.

This marks an important new change in Stravinsky's direction, and it is especially remarkable since it occurred at an age when artists generally tend to fall back and content themselves by consolidating positions they have already won. One cannot withhold admiration from so vigorous a spirit, who on the threshold of his eighth decade has no hesitation in taking over a completely new technique, analysing the principles on which it is based, and finally using it, not merely out of simple curiosity, but as a means of constructing large-scale and important works like the *Canticum Sacrum* of 1956, *Agon* of 1957 and *Threni* of 1958.

This apparent conversion to serialism seemed so surprising at the moment it happened that Stravinsky's supporters took special pains to make it clear that it in no way implied a victory for his rival Schoenberg. This is in fact the sense of the account given by Robert Craft, a young American conductor and critic who after meeting Stravinsky in the summer of 1947 was invited to join his household in Hollywood and became his musical amanuensis. Craft has told us* that it took five years for his own enthusiasm for serial music to win over Stravinsky. It was not until January and February 1952 that as the result of repeated hearings of Webern's Quartet op. 22 the ice was broken. From then on he took pains to familiarise himself with the output—restricted in quantity, but pithy and pregnant in invention—of Schoenberg's young disciple, Webern, who had died so tragically on 15th October, 1945.

A Personal Preface by Robert Craft. *The Score*, June, 1957.

THE NEW ADVENTURE

It was in May 1953 that Stravinsky first met Dylan Thomas, whose poetry he had admired for some time. The two artists conceived a common enthusiasm for the project of a joint opera, which they were to write together as soon as the poet had returned to American from England. Unfortunately this opera was destined never to see the light of day, for hardly had Dylan Thomas returned to New York that autumn than death overtook him; and it was in memory of this all too brief friendship that Stravinsky wrote his *In Memoriam Dylan Thomas*, Dirge-Canons and Song, which contains as its centre-piece a song for tenor and string quartet, in which the principles of serial construction are applied to the setting of a poem Dylan Thomas wrote in memory of his father. This is preceded and followed by two sets of Dirge-Canons set for four trombones alternating with string quartet.

In this score Stravinsky showed that he was fully determined to set out on his new adventure. In it he uses serial methods of construction. The writing is strictly contrapuntal, and there is no filling in for the sake of filling in. The two canons are written in mirror form so that the last is a kind of reflection of the first. The world première was given by the Monday Evening Concerts at Los Angeles on 20th September 1954 with Robert Craft conducting. The first European performance took place in Rome shortly afterwards in the presence of the composer, his second wife Vera and his eldest son Theodore.

It was on the occasion of this trip that the suggestion was made that he should write a work dedicated to St. Mark, the patron saint of Venice; and with this in view a number of acoustic trials were carried out in various Venetian churches. As is well known, St. Mark's itself, which was originally a Roman basilica, has suffered a number of changes at various times—Byzantine adaptations in the eleventh century and Gothic in the fifteenth. It may well be thought that Stravinsky was particularly attracted by a style of architecture which, by virtue of its oriental roots, was closely related to that of the Russian Orthodox Churches where he had worshipped as a boy. In any case, there is a clear connection between the plan of St. Mark's and the musical form of the *Canticum Sacrum ad Honorem Sancti Marci Nominis*, the five parts of which are the symbolic equivalent in sound of the five cupolas of the basilica. Furthermore, there are close links between the musical architecture of the work and the subject on which it is based. For instance, the retrograde form used for the outer movements—*Euntes in mundum* and *Illi autem profecti*—is justified by the fact that the words of the two movements provide a unifying message in the Lord's command to preach the Gospel. As Craft says, 'the first part tells the Lord's command, and the last part its fulfilment, that is to say, the future which has become the past'. In this work there is a symbolic interplay between the subject

and the form which is reminiscent of some of the procedures of the Middle Ages.

The *Canticum Sacrum* was finished in 1955, and the first performance took place in St. Mark's, Venice, on 13th September, 1956, under the composer's direction. The programme was completed by an arrangement of Bach's canonic variations on the Christmas Hymn, *Vom Himmel Hoch da komm'ich her*, specially composed by Stravinsky for the occasion. Although both the *Canticum* and the Symphony of Psalms were inspired by deep religious feelings, they differ from each other both in spirit and in style. If anything, the hieratic severity of the *Canticum* recalls the Mass of 1947

In 1957 Stravinsky celebrated his 75th birthday; and to commemorate this event, the City of Los Angeles decided to devote a special programme to his music in its eleventh annual Musical Festival. This included the first performance of his latest work *Agon* (17th June) which had been commissioned for the New York City Ballet by Lincoln Kirstein, who ten years earlier had also been responsible for commissioning *Orpheus*. The theatrical première of *Agon* took place the following December in New York when the ballet was choreographed for four male and eight female dancers by George Balanchine.

The critics seem to have been rather disconcerted by this abstract ballet, without costumes or scenery, whose Greek title might have been construed as implying some sort of a contest. The stage spectacle, while containing no dramatic element of any kind and avoiding any attempt at literal illustration, aimed at offering a visual counterpart in choreographic terms to the music.

The score contains fifteen numbers. Four distinct groups of dance numbers are separated from each other by a prelude and two interludes. Some of these numbers are inspired by old French dance forms from the sixteenth and seventeenth centuries e.g. *Bransle de Poitou*, *Gailliarde*, and *Sarabande*.

But the time was approaching when Stravinsky was about to astonish the world by a more radical metamorphosis than any of his previous ones.

Stravinsky and Rieti

THE CONJUNCTION OF STRAVINSKY
AND WEBERN

On examining the first Stravinsky scores to use serial technique, such as the Gigue in the Septet and the brief *In Memoriam Dylan Thomas*, it appears that they infringe the essential requirements of dodecaphony (apart from the question of atonal gravity) by their use of cadences, symmetry and repetition in order to create poles of attraction. These elements of polarity are even more evident in his two other works of larger dimensions (17 minutes for the *Canticum*, and 20 for *Agon*). Here it is not so much a question of cadential punctuation or internal effects of symmetry, as of complete musical numbers, used as architectonic features of considerable importance to frame the symphonic movement and ensure its stability by their powerful tonal affirmation. This is fully borne out by Stravinsky's statement to Craft in June 1957: '*The intervals of my series are attracted by tonality; I compose vertically and that is, in one sense at least, to compose tonally*'.[*] In passing let it be said that this is a most controversial assertion: but that is not the question now—what matters is Stravinsky's clear-cut adherence to tonality.

A number of critics have pointed out the contradiction inherent in this belief in tonality combined with respect for the series. *Le Journal Musical Français*, referring to the *Canticum*, called it 'a fresco where every method and idiom, ranging from *bel canto* to serial composition is used in the service of an art that deliberately inclines towards the baroque by reason of its rich decorative properties and inflated though sometimes powerful expressiveness'.[†] M. Antoine Goléa wrote in *L'Express*,[**] that in his view *Agon* suffered 'from a regrettable disparity of writing and style'. On the other hand, a number of Italian critics have recognised *In Memoriam Dylan Thomas* as the starting point of a new art resulting from the fusion of Schoenberg's twelve note serialism and Stravinsky's own polydiatonicism; and this idea was developed by Clauss Henning Bachman, a Viennese critic, in an article he wrote[‡] after attending the first performance of the *Canticum* at Venice.

What is to be thought of these contradictory views? There is much evidence to show that the temper of Stravinsky's musical thought is irreconcilable with the serial process of composition—firstly, because of the actual sonority of the interplay between the different vocal and instrumental lines, and also because of the essential quality of his music.

---

[*]*Conversations with Igor Stravinsky* by Igor Stravinsky and Robert Craft. 1959.

[†]26th November, 1956.

[**]17th October, 1957.

[‡] See *Musika*, July 1955, p. 117.

There is a gramophone record (Vega C 30 A 120) with his *Canticum* on one side and Webern's *Cantata* op. 29 on the other, which is particularly revealing in this respect. A comparison of the two works gives the impression that whereas in the case of Webern the serial idiom has been so completely assimilated as to appear perfectly natural, in the case of Stravinsky, it appears forced and unnatural, and the resulting sonority which in Webern's *Cantata* has clearly been most carefully studied and worked out, seems haphazard and artificial in the *Canticum* rather than the inevitable result of the polyphony. Furthermore, in rejecting the architectonic consequences of serialism, Stravinsky is really showing himself to be opposed to its very spirit, for by this attitude he refuses to allow it to produce its own natural forms. It must be affirmed that the idea of achieving a synthesis of tonal and atonal music, which represent two absolutely irreconcilable worlds, is a chimera. Atonality is a complete system in itself; and the mixture in a single work of two mutually exclusive methods of thought is a contradiction that is bound to create incongruous results.

It may be argued that in the past Stravinsky frequently accustomed his auditors to mixtures of style, and in this case he has recognised that serial music offers another musical element to be assimilated and incorporated in his technique, just as in previous years he took over a theme by Rossini in *A Card Game*, tunes by Schubert and Tchaikovsky in other works, and '*Elle avait une jamb' de bois*' in *Petrushka*.

But, in any case, one thing is certain: by advertising his allegiance, even if only in part, to the cause of serialism, Stravinsky has placed himself firmly and squarely at the crossroads where the two main streams of contemporary music meet today.

Today

Stravinsky and Mr. Fromm leaving the Columbia Studios, New York

Today

Threni, id est lamentationes Jeremiae Prophetae was given its first performance under Stravinsky's direction at Venice in September, 1958. The score, which was completed on 21st March, 1958, is a setting of various extracts from the Lamentations of Jeremiah for six soloists, a mixed choir and a rather large orchestra, which is used very sparingly. The main emphasis is placed on the vocal element, which bristles with difficulties.

A musical analysis of this cantata reveals the complexity of its construction. In this case Stravinsky seems to have completely embraced the tenets of serialism, and the score shows an unrelenting exploitation of its contrapuntal resources, while the use of architectural symmetry, somewhat like the form of responses in the liturgy, helps to give the work cohesion. Important passages allocated to the soloists and distinguished by great rhythmic freedom alternate with choral phrases which are ornamented rather than accompanied by the orchestra. The mechanically regular syllabic treatment of the Latin text delivered *parlando sotto voce* by the chorus in the First Elegy is rather unhappy since it completely cuts across the natural scansion of a language whose suppleness consists largely in the alternation of short and long vowel sounds. In this respect, the composer may rightly be accused of having committed a barbarous crime against rhythm.

Nevertheless, there are many things to admire in this score, such as the canons for men's voices in the Third Elegy—for two voices, three voices, followed by a double canon for four voices—and it is undeniable that throughout he shows that he has acquired great mastery of the serial technique. The tonal passages that played such an important part in the construction of his earlier serial works are completely absent in *Threni*; but traces of diatonicism still remain in certain places like little islands in a swirling atonal flood.

The score is punctuated by strangely articulated cries formed by setting the Hebrew letters that introduce the verses and recall the illuminated initials that are the glory of so many medieval manuscripts.

ALEPH: How doth the city sit solitary, that was full of people! . . .

BETH: She weepeth sore in the night, and her tears are on her cheeks.

RES: Behold, O Lord, for I am in distress: my bowels are troubled; mine heart is turned within me . . . abroad the sword bereaveth, at home there is as death.

This extract from the First Elegy sets the emotional climate of the work —one of extreme spiritual austerity, stripped of any trace of earthy seductiveness. Nevertheless, the texture soon becomes somewhat more animated; and the polyphonic veil is rent asunder in the Third Elegy where the chorus, following the initial calls of the soloists, sings:—

HETH: It is the Lord's mercies that we are not consumed . . .

TETH: The Lord is good unto them that wait for him, to the soul that seeketh him . . .

But these are only the palest of rays; and presently the sky becomes overcast again and everything reverts to darkness and desolation.

Remember, O Lord, what is come upon us;
Consider and behold our reproach.

And even the final words of hope seem to be uttered with deep apprehension.

Turn thou us unto thee, O Lord, and we shall be turned;
renew our days as of old.

Bitter as tears, acrid as ashes, *Threni* is certainly a song of penitence, and in it Stravinsky has produced a grey sunless music that makes an ideal accompaniment to the lamentations of the Old Testament prophet, as he bewails the fate of the Jews and the destruction of the Holy City.

The key to the enigma of Stravinsky and the true significance of his music is to be found in a particular aspect of the creative activity of the great masters of the twentieth century—painters, poets and musicians— which can be summarised as their ability to solve a given problem; and this is closely linked with the intense appetite for discovery that has been

144

*Stravinsky with Balanchine at a
rehearsal of 'Orpheus'*, 1948

characteristic of all forms of contemporary thought. Like the scientific spirit, such creative zest can be turned to constructive purposes only if there is a field for it to explore; similarly, it can be justified only insofar as it tends to create new universes. This problem confronts the artist as well as the composer; and painters like Cézanne, Picasso, Klee and Chagall have tackled it in their own field and according to their own individual talents, as well as composers like Debussy, Ravel, Schoenberg and Stravinsky. In France, in the early years of the twentieth century, there was so strong a desire for novelty that, despite the fact that its explosion shattered the sensitive façade of the school of French music as led by Debussy and Ravel, *The Rite of Spring* was accepted with all its rough and primitive characteristics precisely because it seemed to open up important new musical perspectives. Had anyone tried to swim against this powerful current, he would have seemed to be doing it for a bet or as a challenge. Nevertheless, this is precisely what Stravinsky himself decided to do; and it seemed the most unexpected and para-doxical step imaginable. In fact, the whole of the middle period of his composition is like the registration of a protest against a particular line of development that he suddenly decided showed a dangerously revolutionary tendency although he himself had been one of its main protagonists. While all around him music continued to advance, almost all his own scores from *Mavra* to *The Rake's Progress*, even including such a work as the Symphony in Three Movements, could be regarded as a plea for the return to a tradition whose rules stem from the great works of the past.

But herein lies a strange dramatic irony. This journey through an imaginary museum of music is so unusual that one is bound to reflect upon its true significance. What is the composer looking for? Is it a model that he wants or is he really conducting a search for self-know-ledge? For if there is no universe to discover, there is no real problem to solve. In his wish to forge a new classicism, Stravinsky has confounded tradition with convention. The spirit of his music was truly classical so long as he was creating new forms out of new musical material, but not in *Oedipus Rex* where, misled by a false ideal of simplicity, he produced a score which is a mass of *clichés*.

Deprived of its object the appetite for discovery loses a vital part of its vigour, reverting to a kind of game, while the problem to be solved becomes no more than a simple question of construction.

In his *Poetics of Music* Stravinsky has written 'Once the construction is carried out, and order achieved, everything has been said'—a dogmatic statement that reveals an inordinate belief in the virtues of the will, where-as the act of aesthetic creation does not depend on the excercise of the will or of logic, and in this it shows itself essentially different from the act of scientific invention. This attitude does nothing to explore the ultimate purpose of music and the essential needs that it should satisfy if it is to fulfil its mission of mediating (to use Stravinsky's own expression) between mankind and the material universe in the form of an abstract construction in sound.

In order to understand this, it is sufficient to consider one of Bach's fugues, which are generally held to be the quintessence of pure music. It is self-evident that no composer other than Bach, neither one of his predecessors nor one of his followers, could have written such a piece. To pretend the contrary would be to confer a patent of nobility on all the innumerable obscure musicians who have also written fugues in their lifetime. The difference consists in the fact that Bach has put an essential part of himself into this particular fugue and through it has expressed his serenity, the sincerity of his simple naive religious faith as well as his unique talent. To deny this is tantamount to denying the genius of Bach himself and all the other great musicians, Stravinsky himself included.

Although it may be agreed that music is not necessarily a direct transliteration of emotions, that romanticism and impressionism do not constitute the only ways of contemplating the outside world, and that a work of music can exist on its own quite apart from the presence of any specific subject matter, it does not follow that music can be divorced completely from a certain attitude of mind, from the attachment to a particular being, from a unique mental quality derived from the personality of the composer.

If with the benefit of hindsight, the personality of Stravinsky is re-examined and analysed, it will be seen that he began to turn away from his origins because the enquiring spirit that inhabited his mind started to view matters in a different perspective, seeing them not directly but through western European eyes as part both of the tradition of the past and also of the present; and while key personalities like Cocteau and Picasso play dominating parts in the present, Stravinsky himself remains in some ways outside it. From this it follows that not only has his psychological climate been affected by these diverse influences, some of them close at hand and some of them distant, but also the aesthetic and musical climate in which his works have been conceived and gestated. Although the classicism resulting from this transformation reached an occasional climax, it usually had something forced and un-natural about it and tended at times towards the academic and at others towards the baroque.

Confronted by Stravinsky's recent adoption of serialism, many of his supporters, particularly those who did their best by using one paradox or another to gloss over his weaknesses and justify some of his sudden changes of direction, are likely to reproach him bitterly for a conversion that they regard as a betrayal.

My own view is different. It is of little importance that by reason of this conversion Stravinsky seems to have embraced a creed that formerly he rejected: it is also of little importance that he should impose his own treatment on serialism by remaining—whether voluntarily or involuntarily is not altogether clear—faithful to the principles of tonal polarity, thereby contradicting the fundamental basis of the twelve-tone system of which serialism is only the instrument. To my mind what is of real and enduring importance is the magnificent effort made by the master in his old age to resume his own tradition, which marks the true line of development so far as he is concerned, because it expresses the most significant depths of his thought. By this effort his stature is enhanced, and the whole of his output appears like a vast symphony in three parts, each of which is the outward expression of the vicissitudes of his internal drama.

In the last resort, it is clear that no composer worthy of the name, whatever he does, whatever he pretends to do, is able to divorce himself from his music, because his music, insofar as it is of any value, forms an integral part of himself. The proof is in Stravinsky's work with its thousand different facets, in the many varied manifestations of his talent which can be compared with the thousand incarnations of Buddha. In his many metamorphoses he may appear as a more or less great artist, close to us or quite remote, obscure or radiantly clear; but through all these multifarious aspects we recognise the quintessential genius of the man whom we honour today as Stravinsky.

At the first recording of 'Threni,' New York

Appendices

Chronology

STRAVINSKY

1843   Fedor Ignatevich Stravinsky born, father of Igor.

1873   Fedor Stravinsky engaged at the Kiev Opera.

1876   Fedor Stravinsky engaged at the Imperial Opera House, St. Petersburg.

1882   Igor Stravinsky born at Oranienbaum, near St. Petersburg, on June 5 (Julian Calendar).

1891   Begins to study the piano.

1893   Stravinsky sees Tchaikovsky at the Imperial Opera House.

	1857
Elgar born.	1862
Debussy born	1866
Satie born.	1872
Diaghilev, Scriabin and Vaughan Williams born.	
	1874
Schoenberg born.	1875
Ravel born.	
de Falla born.	
	1881
Bartok and Picasso born.	
	1883
Wagner dies. Webern born.	1884
Debussy's *L'Enfant Prodigue*.	1885
Berg born.	1887
Borodin dies.	1888
Satie's *Gymnopédies*.	
Prokofiev born.	
	1892
Honegger and Milhaud born.	
Tchaikovsky dies.	

1902   Stravinsky meets his future teacher,
            Rimsky-Korsakov. Death of
            Stravinsky's father.

1903   Piano Sonata (unpublished and
                                                        unperformed).

1905   Stravinsky finishes his University
            studies in the spring. In the autumn
            he becomes engaged to his cousin,
            Catherine Nossenko.

Hindemith born.
Richard Strauss's *Till Eulenspiegel*.

1895

Ravel's *La Habanera*.
Brahms dies.
Diaghilev founds *Mir Iskustva*.
Auric and Poulenc born.
Schoenberg's *Die Verklärte Nacht*.

1897

1898
1899

Weill born.
Verdi dies.

1900
1901

Debussy's *Pelléas at Mélisande*.
Walton born.

Russo–Japanese War breaks out.
De Falla's *La Vida Breve*.
Berg becomes a pupil of Schoenberg's.
Diaghilev organises an Exhibition
of Russian Art in Paris.

1904

1906	Marries in January.	*Faun & Shepherdess* (op. 2).
1907	Stravinsky's son Theodore born.	Symphony in Bb(op. 1). Two Melodies (op. 6) (words by Gorodetsky). *Scherzo Fantastique* (op. 3). *Fireworks* (op. 4). *Pastorale.* Four Studies for Piano (op. 7). *Funeral Dirge* (in memoriam Rimsky-Korsakov).
1908	Stravinsky's daughter Ludmilla born.	

Cézanne dies. Shostakovich born.
Picasso's *Les Demoiselles d'Avignon*.
Rimsky-Korsakov's *Kitezh*.
Grieg dies.

1906

Messiaen born.

1908

1909		*The Nightingale* (Act 1).
1910	Visits Paris, La Baule and Clarens. Stravinsky's son Sviatoslav born.	*The Fire Bird.* Two Poems of Verlaine (op. 9).
1911	Stravinsky at Beaulieu. Brief visit to St. Petersburg. Returns to Beaulieu, where he suffers from nicotine poisoning. Joins Diaghilev in Rome and Paris. Returns to Ustilug.	*Petrushka.* Two Poems by Balmont. *The King of the Stars* (Balmont).
1912	Stravinsky visits Paris. Taken by Debussy to hear *Pelléas et Mélisande*. Returns to Ustilug. Visits Bayreuth with Diaghilev to hear *Parsifal*. Settles at Clarens for the winter. Visits Berlin (where he hears Schoenberg's *Pierrot Lunaire*), Budapest and Vienna.	*Three Japanese Lyrics.*

Richard Strauss's *Elektra*.
Schoenberg composes Three Piano
Pieces (op. 11).
Webern composes Six Pieces for
Large Orchestra (op. 6).
First season of Diaghilev's Russian
Ballet in Paris.
Rimsky-Korsakov's *Golden
Cockerel* produced in Moscow.

1909

1910

Balakirev dies.

Strauss's *Der Rosenkavalier*.
Ravel's *L' Heure Espagnole*.
Mahler dies.

1911

Ravel's *Daphnis et Chloé*.

1912

1913
Ravel joins Stravinsky at Clarens for work on *Khovanshchina*. Stravinsky in Paris for first performance of *The Rite of Spring*. Falls ill with typhoid fever. Returns to Ustilug for summer. Settles at Clarens for the winter.

The Rite of Spring.
Three Little Songs
(Souvenir of my Childhood).

1914
Moves temporarily to Leysin because of his wife's illness. Stravinsky's daughter Milena born. Visits Paris for the Russian Ballet season. Settles his family at Salvan (Valais). Visits London, Ustilug, Warsaw, and Kiev. Leaves Salvan for Clarens in the autumn.

Completion of *The Nightingale*.
Three Pieces for String Quartet.
Pribaovtki.
Composition of *The Wedding* begun.

1915
Visits Diaghilev in Florence. Returns to Clarens. Moves to Château d'Oex. Visits Diaghilev in Rome. Settles at Morges. Diaghilev settles (temporarily) at Bellerive, Ouchy. Stravinsky conducts *The Fire Bird* suite at Red Cross gala performances at Geneva and Paris.

Three Easy Pieces for Piano Duet.
Berceuses du Chat.

1916
Visits the Princess de Polignac. Collaboration with Ramuz. Meets Diaghilev at Madrid on his return from America.

1917
Visits Diaghilev in Rome and Naples. Meets Picasso. Summer at Les Diablerets. Death of his brother Gury on the Rumanian front.

Reynard.
Five Easy Pieces for Piano Duet.
Three Children's Tales.
Saucers.
Song of the Volga Boatmen (orchestration
The Song of the Nightingale.

THE OTHERS

Ravel's Poèmes de Mallarmé.
Cocteau dedicates *Le Potomak* to
Stravinsky.
Benjamin Britten born.

HUITIÈME SAISON DES BALLETS RUSSES

Mlle SCHOLLAR, M. LUDKEY et Mme KARSAVINA dans une scène de ballet "JEUX"

Prokofiev's *Ala and Lolly*.
Berg's Three Pieces for Orchestra (op. 6).
Outbreak of the First World War.
Liadov dies.
Dylan Thomas born.

1913

Debussy dedicates one of his three
pieces for two pianos, *En Blanc et
Noir*, to Stravinsky.
Scriabin dies.

1914

1915

1916

Russian Revolution.
Satie's *Parade*.

COMOEDIA

NIJINSKI dans l'"Après-Midi d'un Faune"

1917

1918	Collaborates with Ramuz on *The Soldier's Tale*. Tour cancelled because of influenza epidemic. Stravinsky finishes the composition of *Ragtime* at the moment of the Armistice (11 a.m. on November 11).	Completion of the composition of *The Wedding*. *The Soldier's Tale*. *Ragtime*. Four Russian Songs.
1919	Visits Diaghilev in Paris.	Three Pieces for Clarinet Solo. *Piano-Rag-Music. Pulcinella*.
1920	Leaves Morges and settles in France, first at Carantec and then at Garches.	Concertino for String Quartet. Symphonies of Wind Instruments (dedicated to the memory of Debussy)
1921	Visits Paris, Madrid, London and Anglet. Settles at Biarritz.	*The Five Fingers*. *Suite* (No. 2) for small orchestra (orchestral version of four of the Easy Pieces for Piano Duet). Three Movements of *Petrushka* (piano transcription).
1922	Visits Monte Carlo, Paris and Berlin.	*Mavra*.
1923	Visits Monte Carlo, Paris, Weimar.	Instrumentation of *The Wedding*, *Pastorale* and *Tilimbom*. Octet for Wind Instruments.

Debussy dies.
Bartok's *Blue-Beard's Castle*.
Cocteau's *Le Coq et l'Arlequin*.
End of the First World War.
Puccini's *Trittico*.

Prokofiev's *Chout*.
Honegger's *Le Roi David*.
Diaghilev revives *The Sleeping
Beauty* at the Alhambra, London.
Janacek's *Katya Kabanova*.

Cocteau's *Antigone*.

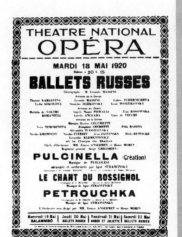

1918

1919

1920

1921

1922

1923

1924   Tours Antwerp, Brussels, Barcelona   Concerto for Piano and Wind
        and Madrid, as conductor of his   Orchestra.
        works. Visits Paris. Plays the solo   Sonata for Piano.
        part in his Piano Concerto. Visits
        Copenhagen. Settles at Nice.

1925   Concert tour of Warsaw, Prague,   Serenade in A (for piano).
        Leipzig, Berlin, Amsterdam, the   *Suite No.* 1 for small orchestra
        Hague, Geneva, Lausanne, Marseilles.   (orchestral version of the four
        First tour of the United States (New   remaining Easy Pieces for Piano Duet)
        York, Boston, Chicago, Philadelphia,
        Cleveland, Detroit, Cincinnati).
        Visits Barcelona, Rome and Paris
        on his return. Plays his Piano
        Sonata at the I.S.C.M. Festival at
        Venice. Concert tour of Zurich,
        Basle, Wiesbaden, Berlin,
        Frankfurt-am-Main, and Copenhagen.

Schoenberg's *Serenade* (op. 24).

Deaths of Satie, Busoni, Fauré and Puccini.
Boulez born.
Berg's *Wozzeck*.
Schoenberg's *Serenade* (op. 24).

STRAVINSKY   COMPOSITIONS

1926   Collaboration with Cocteau
        (*Oedipus Rex*). Concert tour of
        Amsterdam, Rotterdam, Haarlem,
        Budapest, Vienna and Zagreb.
        Conducts *The Nightingale* at the
        Scala, Milan.

1927   Visits London in the summer.   *Oedipus Rex.*

1928   Visits Berlin. Appears at concerts
        in Paris, Barcelona, Rome, Amsterdam   *Apollo Musagetes.*
        and London. Conducts first   *The Fairy's Kiss.*
        performance of *Apollo Musagetes*
        for the Russian Ballet. Spends
        summer at Echarvines. Conducts the
        first performance of *The Fairy's Kiss.*

1929   Appears at concerts in Dresden,   *Capriccio* for piano and orchestra.
        Paris, Berlin. Spends summer at   Four Studies for orchestra
        Echarvines. Plays solo part in his   (Orchestral versions of the Three
        Capriccio.   Pieces for String Quartet and the
                                                    Study for Pianola).

1930   Plays the *Capriccio* in Berlin,   *Symphony of Psalms.*
        Leipzig, Bucharest, Prague and
        Winterthur. Conducts concerts at
        Dusseldorf, Brussels and Amsterdam.
        Spends summer at Charavines.
        Autumn tour of Basle, Zurich,
        Lausanne, Geneva, Berlin, Vienna,
        Mainz, Wiesbaden, Bremen, Munich,
        Nuremberg, Frankfurt-am-Main,
        Mannheim, Brussels, Amsterdam.

Puccini's *Turandot*.
Hindemith's *Cardillac*.
Shostakovich's *First Symphony*.

Weill's *Die Dreigroschenoper*.

Diaghilev dies.

Webern's Quartet (op. 22).
W. H. Auden's *Poems*.

	STRAVINSKY	COMPOSITIONS
1931	Plays the *Capriccio* in Paris and London. Settles at Voreppe (Isère). Visits Oslo. Conducts first performance of Violin Concerto in Berlin, (Dushkin: soloist). Tours Frankfurt-am-Main, London, Cologne, Hanover, Halle, Darmstadt, Paris.	Concerto in D for Violin and Orchestra.
1932	Conducts concerts in Antwerp, Florence, Milan, Berlin. Piano and violin recital tour with Dushkin to Danzig, Paris, Munich, London and Winterthur. Other concerts in Königsberg, Hamburg, Ostrava, Paris, Budapest, Milan, Turin, Rome.	*Duo Concertante*. Various works transcribed for violin and piano.
1933	Meets Gide at Wiesbaden. Spanish concert tour (autumn). Stravinsky's son, Sviatoslav, makes his concert debut at Barcelona as soloist in the *Capriccio* with Stravinsky conducting.	
1934	Visits Copenhagen. Concert tour of Lithuania and Latvia with Dushkin. Conducts first performance of *Persephone* at the Opéra, Paris. Visits London.	*Persephone*.
1935	Second American tour. First performance of the Concerto for Two Solo Pianos given by Stravinsky and his son, Sviatoslav, in the Salle Gaveau, Paris. Visits Bournemouth.	Concerto for Two Solo Pianos. First volume of *Chroniques de ma Vie* published.

Walton's *Belshazzar's Feast.*
Hindemith's *Das Unaufhörliche.*

1931

1932

The burning of the Reichstag, Berlin.
Schoenberg leaves Europe for the
United States.

THÉATRE PIGALLE

CONCERTS SIOHAN
4ᵉ CONCERT

Samedi 20 Décembre, à 17 h.

IGOR
STRAWIN/KY

jouera son Concerto *pour piano et orchestre*

Pétrouchka (4ᵉ tableau) . . . **STRAWINSKY**
Pulcinella . . . . —
Concerto pour piano et
orchestre . . . . —
Au piano : l'Auteur
L'Oiseau de Feu . . . . . —

Chef d'orchestre : **ROBERT SIOHAN**

Places de 10 à 50 francs – Corbeille, 60 fr.
LOCATION : Théâtre Pigalle (Trud. 94-50 · Durand — Eschig

1933

1934

Elgar dies.
Shostakovitch's *Lady Macbeth of Mtsensk.*
Dylan Thomas's 18 *Poems.*

1935

Berg dies.

	STRAVINSKY	COMPOSITIONS
1936	Acquires French nationality. Unsuccessful in his attempt to be elected a member of the Académie Française.	Second volume of *Chroniques de ma Vie* published. *A Card Game.*
1937	Third visit to America. Conducts first performance of *A Card Game* at the Metropolitan Opera New York. Visits London in autumn.	
1938	Death of Stravinsky's daughter Ludmilla.	*Dumbarton Oaks* Concerto.
1939	Deaths of Stravinsky's mother and wife. Stravinsky leaves France for the United States. Delivers the Charles Eliot Norton lectures at Harvard University.	*Poetics of Music.*
1940	Marries Vera de Bosset at Boston. Settles in Hollywood.	Symphony in C. *Tango.*

Roussel dies.

Ravel dies.

Auden leaves England for America.
Britten leaves England for America.
Outbreak of Second World War.

Bartok leaves Hungary for America.

Paul Bunyan (words by Auden; music
by Britten) produced in New York.

1942		*Danses Concertantes.* *Circus Polka.* *Four Norwegian Moods.*
1943		*Ode.*
1944	Stravinsky finishes the composition of *Scènes de Ballet* at the moment the news of the liberation of Paris reaches him.	Sonata for Two Pianos. *Scènes de Ballet.* *Scherzo à la Russe.* *Babel. Elegy.*
1945	Acquires American nationality	Symphony in Three Movements. *Ebony Concerto.*
1946		Concerto in D for strings.
1947	Enters into correspondence with Robert Craft.	Revised versions of *Petrushka* and of many early compositions.

1941

Britten leaves America for England.   1942

1943

1944

1945

End of Second World War.
Britten's *Peter Grimes*. Webern dies.

1946

de Falla dies.

1947

1948	Auden delivers the libretto of *The Rake's Progress*. Craft joins the Stravinsky household in Hollywood.	*Orpheus.* *Mass.*
1951	Stravinsky visits Europe and conducts first performance of *The Rake's Progress* at the Fenice, Venice.	*The Rake's Progress.*
1952	Stravinsky studies Webern's Quartet op. 22 and various works of Schoenberg. Visits Europe.	*Cantata.*
1953	Meets Dylan Thomas in Boston (May) and plans to write an opera with him.	*Septet.* *Three Songs from William Shakespeare.*
1954		*In Memoriam Dylan Thomas* (Dirge-Canons and Song).
1956	Visits Europe and conducts first performance of the *Canticum Sacrum* in St. Mark's, Venice.	*Canticum Sacrum.*
1957	First performance of *Agon* in Los Angeles on June 17 at a concert to celebrate his 75th birthday. Visits Dartington, Devon, for the Summer School of Music.	*Agon.*
1958	Visits Europe and conducts the first performance of *Threni* in the Scuola di San Rocco, Venice.	*Threni.*

Bartok dies.
Messiaen's *Turangalila—Symphonie*.

1949
Strauss dies.
Schoenberg dies.

1951

1952

Prokofiev dies.
Dylan Thomas dies in New York
(November).   1953

1954

Honegger dies.
Boulez's *Le Marteau*   1955
sans Maître.

Britten's *Noye's Fludde*.
Vaughan Williams dies.

	STRAVINSKY	COMPOSITIONS
1959	Visits Japan.	*Movements* for piano and orchestra. *Double Canon* for String Quartet. *Epitaphium* for flute, clarinet and harp.
1960	Visits South America. Conducts first performance of *Movements* in New York.	*Conversations with Igor Stravinsky* published. *Monumentum pro Gesualdo di Venosa ad CD Annum* (three madrigals re-composed for instruments by Stravinsky). *Tres Sacrae Cantiones* of Gesualdo, completed by Stravinsky. *Memories and Commentaries* published.
1961	Visits Europe, Africa and Australia.	*A Sermon, a Narrative and a Prayer*
1962	Visits Africa, Europe, Israel and the U.S.S.R., conducting numerous concerts to celebrate his 80th birthday.	Anthem ('The dove descending breaks the air'). *The Flood.* *Expositions and Developments* published.
1963	Visits Germany, Czechoslovakia, Hungary, Jugoslavia, France, Norway, England, Ireland, Italy, Brazil, Sicily.	*Abraham and Isaac* *Dialogues and a Diary* published.
1964	Visits Israel and Germany. Conducts *Symphony of Psalms* in England.	*Elegy for J.F.K.* *Variations (Aldous Huxley in Memoriam)*
1965	Visits France, Switzerland, Poland. Conducts *The Fire Bird* in England.	*Introitus*
1966		*Requiem Canticles* *The Owl and the Pussycat* *Themes and Episodes* published.
1968	Visits Switzerland and France. Performance of the incomplete and final versions of *The Wedding* in Los Angeles.	Instrumentation of *Two Songs of Hugo Wolf.*
1969		Arrangement of *Two Preludes and Fugues* by Bach.

A Selected Bibliography

Adam, J., *Impressions Françaises en Russie*. Paris, Hachette, 1912.

Apollinaire, G., *Le Flaneur des Deux Rives*. Paris, Edition de la Sirène, 1920.

Ansermet, E., *Les Contemporains*. Geneva, Edition Mazenod, 1946.

Beck, G., *Darius Milhaud, Etude*. Heugel & Cie, 1949.

Boretz, Benjamin and Edward T. Cone (eds.), *Perspectives on Schoenberg and Stravinsky*. Princeton, Princeton University Press, 1969.

Casella, A., *Strawinski*. Brescia, Editrice 'La Scuola', 1951.

Cocteau, J., *Le Coq et l'Arlequin*. Paris, Edition de la Sirène, 1918.

Collaer, P., *Stravinsky*. Brussels, Editions 'Equilibres', 1930.

Corle, E. (ed.), *Igor Stravinsky: A Merle Armitage Book*. New York, Duell, Sloan & Pearce, 1949.

Fleischer, H., *Strawinsky*. Berlin, Russischer Musik Verlag, 1931.

Lang, Paul Henry (ed.), *Stravinsky: a new appraisal of his work*. New York, The Norton Library, 1963.

Lederman, M. (ed.), *Stravinsky in the Theatre*. London, Peter Owen Ltd., 1951.

Lifar, S., *Serge Diaghilev*. London, Putnam, 1940.

Malipiero, G. F., *Strawinsky*. Venice, Cavillino, 1945.

Meylan, Pierre, *Une Amitié Célèbre: C. F. Ramuz/Igor Stravinsky*. Lausanne, Editions du Cervin, 1961.

Nabokov, Nicolas, *Igor Stravinsky*. Berlin, Colloquium Verlag, 1964.

Oleggini, L., *Connaissance de Stravinsky*. Lausanne, M. P. Foetisch, 1952.

Paoli, D. de', *Igor Strawinsky*. Turin, Paravia, 1934.

Ramuz, C. F., *Souvenirs sur Igor Stravinsky*. Lausanne, Editions Mermod, 1929.

Rimsky-Korsakov, N., *Memoirs of My Musical Life*. New York, Knopf, 1942.

Schaeffner, A., *Strawinsky*. Paris, Editions Rieder, 1931.

Schloezer, B. de, *Igor Stravinsky*. Paris, Editions Claude Aveline, 1929.

Schoenberg, A., *Style and Idea*. London, Williams & Norgate, 1951.

Stravinsky, I., *Chronicle of My Life*. Translated from the French. London, Gollancz, 1936; New York, Simon and Schuster, 1936 (under the title *An Autobiography*).

Stravinsky, I., *Poetics of Music: in the form of six lessons*. Translated from the French by Arthur Knodel and Ingolf Dahl. Cambridge, Harvard University Press, 1947.

Stravinsky, I., *The Rite of Spring: Sketches, 1911 – 1913* (facsimile reproductions from the autographs). London, Boosey & Hawkes, 1969.

Stravinsky, I. and Craft, R., *Conversations with Igor Stravinsky*. New York, Doubleday, 1959; London, Faber and Faber, 1959.

Stravinsky, I. and Craft, R., *Memories and Commentaries*. New York, Doubleday, 1960; Faber and Faber, 1960.

Stravinsky, I. and Craft, R., *Expositions and Developments*. New York, Doubleday, 1962; London, Faber and Faber, 1962.

Stravinsky, I. and Craft, R., *Dialogues and a Diary*. New York, Doubleday, 1963; London, Faber and Faber, 1968.

Stravinsky, I. and Craft, R., *Themes and Episodes*. New York, Knopf, 1966.

Strawinsky, T., *The Message of Igor Strawinsky*. Translated from the French by Robert Craft and André Marion. London, Boosey & Hawkes, 1953.

Strobel, H., *Igor Strawinsky*. Zurich, Atlantis Verlag, 1956.

Tansman, A., *Igor Stravinsky*. Paris, Amiot-Dumont, 1948.

Vlad, R., *Stravinsky*. Translated from the Italian by Frederick and Ann Fuller. London, Oxford University Press, 1960.

White, E. W., *Stravinsky: The Composer and His Works*. London, Faber and Faber, 1966; Berkeley and Los Angeles, University of California Press, 1966.

Iconography

Illustrations are reproduced here with the kind permission of Éditions du Seuil, from the following sources: Associated Press, Bibliothèque Nationale, Bibliothèque de l'Opéra, Bulloz, Cartier-Bresson/Magnum, Giraudon, Jacqueline Hyde, Galerie Louise Leiris, Lipnitzki, Coll. Jean Marabini, Inge Morath/Magnum, Les Reporters Associés, Éditions du Rocher, Coll. Siohan, Roger Viollet, Sabine Weiss/Rapho. Particular thanks are due to Madame Dugardin, Monsieur André Meyer and Monsieur Theodore Stravinsky for allowing the reproduction of documents in their possession.

Browsing at the bouquinistes by the Seine, 1923 (reproduced from 'Conversations avec Stravinsky', edited by du Recher)